GUIDING WORD

VOLUME 3

The Books of Wisdom and Poetry

CONCORDIA PUBLISHING HOUSE · SAINT LOUIS

3558 S. Jefferson Ave., St. Louis, MO 63118-3968
1-800-325-3040 • cph.org

Illustrations by Dede Putra

Portions of this book have been compiled from, adapted from, and inspired by various sources, including *The Lutheran Study Bible*, Concordia Publishing House, 2009; the Concordia Commentary series, Concordia Publishing House, 1996–; *Lutheran Bible Companion*, vol. 1, Concordia Publishing House, 2014; and *Concordia's Complete Bible Handbook for Students*, Concordia Publishing House, 2011.

Manufactured in China/064630/340862

Library of Congress Cataloging-in-Publication Data

Title: The Books of Wisdom and Poetry : guiding word.

Description: Saint Louis : Concordia Publishing House, 2024- | Series: The guiding word ; volume 3 | Summary: "This six-volume series will take readers through each book of the Bible, showing the unified narrative of God's plan of salvation. Using this resource, readers will (1) understand the history of God's people and His promise; (2) gain a basic grasp of each book of the Bible; (3) see Jesus' saving mission in each book of the Bible; and (4) develop fundamental Bible reading and interpretation skills"-- Provided by publisher.

Identifiers: LCCN 2022060172 (print) | LCCN 2022060173 (ebook) | ISBN 9780758671929 (v. 3 ; paperback) | ISBN 9780758671936 (v. 3 ; ebook)

Subjects: LCSH: Bible Old Testament--Introductions.

Classification: LCC BS1140.3 .B66 2024 (print) | LCC BS1140.3 (ebook) | DDC 221.6--dc23/eng/20230621

LC record available at https://lccn.loc.gov/2022060172

LC ebook record available at https://lccn.loc.gov/2022060173

---

1 2 3 4 5 6 7 8 9 10 34 33 32 31 30 29 28 27 26 25

TABLE OF CONTENTS

Welcome v

Job 1

Psalms 33

Proverbs 133

Ecclesiastes 159

Song of Solomon 181

Welcome

Welcome to *Guiding Word*. This six-volume collection will help you better read and understand the Bible, the most important book ever written. In it, we read and hear God's Word, which is written so that we may believe that Jesus is the Christ, and that by believing we may have eternal life in His name (John 20:31).

Why have another Bible resource? First, the Bible is a complex library of books, and it is often intimidating for people to read on their own. Second, while there are many resources designed to help you read and understand the Bible, each has its own format and style and may not be suitable for every learner. We hope this resource will fill a gap and be useful for you.

Think of this series of books as a travel guide to the Bible. Just as a travel guide helps you prepare for and better enjoy a trip, this resource will enable you to better understand and appreciate the Bible as you journey through it. The sections have been designed to help you prepare for reading and understanding difficult passages, to explain the overall course of the Scriptures, to prompt you to reflect on the text as you read, to point out important milestones and events, and to guide you to Jesus' presence throughout the Bible.

If you are already familiar with the organization of the Bible, feel free to skip ahead to the section titled "What's in *Guiding Word*?"

What's in the Bible?

The Bible is all about God's plan to restore fallen humanity and His broken creation by sending His Son. But what's in the Bible? How do we look at it? How do we use it? Though we call the Bible a book, it's actually a collection of sixty-six books. These were written over a period of 1,500 years by many authors.

The Bible has two divisions: the Old Testament and the New Testament. We don't use the word *testament* too often today. It's related to words like *covenant* and *contract*.

The Old Testament includes the first thirty-nine books of the Bible. These are the books written about the events that happened before Jesus was born. They all point us toward Jesus. The name *Old Testament* is a little misleading because sometimes we think of old things as not important or out of style. Instead, these books can be thought of as the first covenant or promise that God made to His people to send the Savior, Jesus. And as you will see, Jesus is present throughout the Old Testament. The New Testament includes the last twenty-seven books of the Bible, which record Jesus' life and mission, as well as the life of Jesus' early followers in the church. These books point us back to Jesus and how He fulfilled all of God's promises made for us in the Old Testament. Again, these are all about Jesus.

The books of the Bible are organized in a way that may seem confusing at first but makes sense when you know the system. How are the books in a library organized? In libraries, books are organized by their type. Fiction is in one section, and nonfiction is in another; magazines are in one spot and children's books in another. The same goes for the Bible. Instead of the books being ordered by the date they were written or by their authors, the books of the Bible are put in categories, or genres; then the books are generally organized by date written within that genre.

Navigating the Library

The first five books of the Old Testament—Genesis, Exodus, Leviticus, Numbers, and Deuteronomy—are called the Books of Moses, or the Torah, meaning "Law of God." They were written down by Moses and are covered in the first volume of this series.

The next books in the Old Testament are called the Books of History. These tell the history of God's people from the time of Moses up to the time of Jesus and are covered in the second volume.

Next are the Books of Wisdom and Poetry. These poetical books were written at different times during the Old Testament history, mostly by kings David and Solomon. These are covered in the third volume.

The last group of Old Testament books are the Books of the Prophets. These books record God's special messages to His Old Testament people, mostly during the second half of their history. They are discussed in the fourth volume.

The New Testament has five genres. The first four books—Matthew, Mark, Luke, and John—are called the Gospels. Each Gospel tells of the life and mission of Jesus from a different writer and perspective. These accounts make up the heart of the Bible and are covered in the fifth *Guiding Word* volume.

Next is the book of the Acts of the Apostles (also known simply as Acts). This historical book records events from the early years of the Christian Church and the lives of the first Christians after Jesus ascended into heaven. The next books are called the Pauline Epistles (*epistle* means "letter"). These are letters that the apostle Paul wrote to the early Christians. Near the end of the New Testament are the General Epistles. These are letters that other people besides Paul wrote to the early Christians. The final book of the Bible is the only book of prophecy in the New Testament, the book of Revelation. This shows the vision Jesus revealed to the apostle John about life in the end times (that is, the time between Christ's first and second coming) and the restoration of God's creation. The books of Acts through Revelation are covered in the sixth and final volume of *Guiding Word*.

66 BOOKS OF THE BIBLE

OLD TESTAMENT	
BOOKS OF MOSES *(Torah)*	GENESIS, EXODUS, LEVITICUS, NUMBERS, DEUTERONOMY
HISTORY	JOSHUA, JUDGES, RUTH, 1 SAMUEL, 2 SAMUEL, 1 KINGS, 2 KINGS, 1 CHRONICLES, 2 CHRONICLES, EZRA, NEHEMIAH, ESTHER
WISDOM & POETRY	JOB, PSALMS, PROVERBS, ECCLESIASTES, SONG OF SOLOMON
PROPHETS	ISAIAH, JEREMIAH, LAMENTATIONS, EZEKIEL, DANIEL, HOSEA, JOEL, AMOS, OBADIAH, JONAH, MICAH, NAHUM, HABAKKUK, ZEPHANIAH, HAGGAI, ZECHARIAH, MALACHI
NEW TESTAMENT	
GOSPELS	MATTHEW, MARK, LUKE, JOHN
HISTORY	ACTS
PAULINE EPISTLES *(Letters)*	ROMANS, 1 CORINTHIANS, 2 CORINTHIANS, GALATIANS, EPHESIANS, PHILIPPIANS, COLOSSIANS, 1 THESSALONIANS, 2 THESSALONIANS, 1 TIMOTHY, 2 TIMOTHY, TITUS, PHILEMON
GENERAL EPISTLES	HEBREWS, JAMES, 1 PETER, 2 PETER, 1 JOHN, 2 JOHN, 3 JOHN, JUDE
END TIMES	REVELATION

Navigating the Bible

When you open up a Bible, you'll see chapter and verse numbers scattered throughout the pages. Did you know that those numbers were not originally there? As people used the Bible more and more and made copies, later scholars eventually put in these numbers to help people quickly find sections or passages. We call these Bible references.

UNDERSTANDING BIBLE REFERENCES

The following diagram illustrates how a common Bible reference to **John 3:16** breaks down.

Book Title	Chapter Number	Verse Number
John	3:	16

Using the Bible's table of contents, look up the book of John. Then find chapter 3 and finally verse 16.

What's in *Guiding Word*?

Each volume of *Guiding Word* is laid out in a similar fashion. After this series introduction is an introduction for that specific volume. Then, each book of the Bible has its own introduction, which will help you better understand and dig into that particular book.

Each book of the Bible follows an outline, which breaks the book into major divisions and then each division into sections. The section heads were not included in the original biblical text but were added later to help clarify how the text flows from narrative to narrative or idea to idea. In *Guiding Word*, these correspond to the subheadings in the ESV translation of the Bible. From here on out, we will refer to these subhead sections as "passages."

Following the pattern of a travel guide, *Guiding Word* includes some features to help you read through, better understand, and reflect on each passage of the Bible. These features include the following:

(1) **Orientation.** This is a short summary of each passage. Just as a travel guide gives you a glimpse of where you will be going on your journey before you arrive, the summary will help orient you to where you are in the Bible and where you are going. After reading the summary for each passage, read the text itself in your Bible. Alternatively, if you are skimming a book of the Bible, previewing the book, or only want to understand the high points before reading deeper, these summaries are a good place to start.

(2) **Observation Points.** In the side margins, you will find open-ended questions. Use these reflection questions to help you slow down, observe, and reflect on the passage. There is room in the side margin for recording reflections, thoughts, and notes as you go. Just as a travel guide will prompt you to look out for specific things on your way, the reflection questions will help you better observe what's going on in the text.

(3) **Landmarks.** These special features, interspersed in the text, will help you appreciate the overall journey through God's Word. In any journey, you will encounter landmarks of all types that pop out to you, may interest you, or may even make you scratch your head. Landmarks in *Guiding Word* are identified by icons and colored bars, and can be read before or after you read the corresponding passage. Landmarks include the following categories:

VISUALIZE

This feature includes maps, diagrams, pictures, or infographics to help you visualize scenes, locations, and concepts in a passage.

PICTURE OF THE SAVIOR

This Old Testament feature highlights people, places, or events that set the stage for the coming of Jesus and help reveal His work of salvation.

LINK BETWEEN THE TESTAMENTS

In the Old Testament, this highlights people or events that Jesus or His apostles will discuss, explain, or fulfill in the New Testament. In the New Testament, this feature points the reader back to the Old Testament person or event that set the stage for the New Testament passage.

CLEAR THE CONFUSION

This Landmark clarifies passages that are likely to leave the reader confused and fills the gaps—providing backstories, describing future developments, or discussing the significance of the event.

SET THE SCENE

This feature explains important cultural or historical themes that help you better understand the context of the passage.

WAYPOINT

This feature is designed to be a longer stopping point. When you travel, you will likely stop at notable locations for an extended period of time to really experience the destination. Waypoints in *Guiding Word* function like stopping points that are worth investigating along the journey through God's Word. Each Waypoint has a three-part structure:

- What does this text show us?
- What does this text reveal about God's plan of salvation?
- What does this text uncover about our identity and calling as God's people today?

Each Waypoint also has reflection questions associated with it. The Waypoints can be considered on your own or in a group study. However you choose to use the Waypoints is up to you, but use the summaries and reflection prompts to help guide you through a deeper reading of the text.

How to Use *Guiding Word*

You can use this resource in multiple ways:

- Read through the Bible on your own, passage by passage. The summary of each passage will help orient you to where the narrative is taking you, and the reflection questions are observation prompts that will help you pay closer attention to what you're reading. The interspersed Landmark features will help you visualize important images or concepts, or understand and connect key themes to the overall story of Scripture.
- Read through the Bible in a small group or Bible study setting. The guided summaries and reflection questions make good prompts if you are reading through the Scriptures as a group, providing some reflections along the way. The Waypoint sections also serve as great places to stop and reflect on key narratives.
- Read a good thirty-thousand-foot summary of the Bible. *Guiding Word* includes summaries of passages, and if you have never read certain books of the Bible or are intimidated by their length, you can take a few minutes to get introduced or oriented to them via summaries and graphics.

Whether or not you've read through all or parts of the Bible before, *Guiding Word* will serve as your companion and guide through the journey.

The Books of Wisdom and Poetry

The five Old Testament books covered in this third volume of *Guiding Word* are very different in character from the historical books covered in the first two volumes. They take us deep into the lives of God's people, inside their hearts and minds as they struggle to understand living as God's people in this sin-stained world. In the pages of Job, Psalms, Proverbs, Ecclesiastes, and the Song of Solomon, God's people not only wrestle with familiar issues of suffering, persecution, and betrayal but also find joy, hope, peace, and comfort from God's promises and deliverance.

Journeying Through the Books of Wisdom and Poetry

The book of Job was written between the time of Abraham and that of Moses. As Job goes from prosperity to poverty and deep suffering, he and his friends try to determine God's place in human suffering. We feel the pain and despair of Job's suffering, and then we are lifted up in hope as Job declares, "I know that my Redeemer lives" (Job 19:25). Finally, God answers Job from a whirlwind, teaching us to view suffering from a true perspective.

The book of Psalms has been called the hymnbook of the Old Testament. The 150 psalms cover the wide range of human experience but always bring us back to God, our joy and our comforter. Several psalms teach God's people about the life and work of the coming Messiah.

The book of Proverbs is a collection of wisdom sayings—some short, some extended studies. They all emphasize the wisdom of living in the fear of God—remembering God is our Creator, our Savior, and our Judge, we are wise to live by His Word in humility and repentance.

Ecclesiastes puts our earthly lives in perspective, showing the vanity of the sinful desires that entice us to indulge them and abandon God's way of life. The book teaches us the secret to finding peace, joy, and fulfillment in this brief earthly life.

The Song of Solomon closes this section of the Bible with beautiful poetry that celebrates God's gift of marital love and helps us better understand the great love God has for us and the relationship He seeks with each of His children.

The Books of Wisdom and Poetry, with Their General Divisions

- **Job**
  - Introduction and Satan's Challenge (1:1–2:13)
  - Dialogues Between Job and His Friends (3:1–26:14)
  - Job's Monologues (27:1–31:40)
  - Elihu's Speeches (32:1–37:24)
  - The Lord Speaks and Job Responds (38:1–42:9)
  - God Restores Job (42:10–17)
- **Psalms**
  - Book One, Mostly Personal Psalms of David (1–41)
  - Book Two, Mostly Psalms of David About the Kingdom (42–72)
  - Book Three, Mostly Nationalistic Psalms of Asaph and the Sons of Korah (73–89)
  - Book Four, Mostly Anonymous Psalms and Laments (90–106)
  - Book Five, Mostly Songs of Ascents and Praise (107–150)
- **Proverbs**
  - Introduction and Discourses on Wisdom (1:1–9:18)
  - The Proverbs of Solomon (10:1–22:16)
  - Proverbs from Wise People (22:17–24:34)
  - Solomon's Proverbs Recorded by Hezekiah (25:1–29:27)
  - Agur's Proverbs (30:1–33)
  - King Lemuel's Proverbs and a Poem About an Ideal Wife (31:1–31)

- **Ecclesiastes**
    - All Is Vanity (1:1–2:26)
    - The March of Time (3:1–4:16)
    - Fear of the Lord and Wisdom (5:1–8:17)
    - Death and Living a Godly Life (9:1–12:14)
- **Song of Solomon**
    - The Marriage Union in Four Cycles (1:1–5:1)
    - The Reunion in Married Love (5:2–8:14)

How to Read Hebrew Poetry

Distinguishing Poetry from Prose in English Bibles

We encountered Hebrew poetry in the Books of Moses and the Books of History. Poetry and prose stand side by side in the account of Israel crossing the Red Sea in Exodus 14 and 15. Exodus 14 is a prose account describing God parting the waters and Israel passing through. Exodus 15 is a poetic song Moses wrote for the Israelites to remember what they saw and felt during God's great deliverance.

Prose most often engages the mind, while poetry like we will encounter in the Books of Wisdom and Poetry engages the heart and the imagination.

Parallelism

Instead of rhyme or cadence, Hebrew poetry features parallelism—that is, pairs of words, thoughts, sounds, or forms of grammar that can either complement, compare, or contrast two ideas. When you see Hebrew poetry, look for these parallels to help you understand the meaning of the text.

JOB

Welcome to Job

What do you know of the book of Job? What answers do you hope to learn about human suffering?

It seems easy to fear, love, and trust in God when everything is going well. But what happens when the bottom drops out and we lose everything? How can we fear, love, and trust in God above all things then?

When Satan comes before God in the days of Job's prosperity, he uses this very question to accuse Job: "Does Job fear God for no reason? . . . But stretch out Your hand and touch all that he has, and he will curse You to Your face" (1:9, 11). So God permitted Satan to take Job's possessions and his children's lives. Then he took Job's health. From then on, Job and his friends wrestled with the question "How can we fear, love, and trust in God above all things?" The world similarly accuses believers today. "Why do you trust God? Do you believe only because you are looking for a prosperous life?"

Martin Luther wrote that the book of Job was written for the comfort of believers. Instead of the justice we deserve from God, we receive His grace and mercy. Watch for this theme of God's mercy for His faithful followers as you study the book of Job, and consider these questions: why and how do we trust in God's promise of salvation, fulfilled in the person and work of Jesus Christ?

Job at a Glance

- **Start:** The book of Job begins by describing Job's character and Satan's challenge concerning Job's faithfulness.
- **End:** The book of Job concludes with God restoring Job's fortunes and richly blessing him.
- **Theme:** The Lord shows His mercy and care for His people through His Son, Jesus Christ, even when we fail to trust Him because of our suffering.
- **Author and Date:** Job or one of his contemporaries recorded this book, which was written in the late third or early second millennium BC, around the time of the patriarchs Abraham, Isaac, and Jacob, or the time of Moses.

- **Places Visited:** The entirety of Job takes place in the land of Uz, east of Canaan, in either modern-day Syria or Jordan.
- **Journey Time:** The forty-two chapters of Job can be read in approximately one and three-fourths hours.
- **Outline:**
    - Introduction and Satan's Challenge (1:1–2:13)
    - Dialogues Between Job and His Friends (3:1–26:14)
    - Job's Monologues (27:1–31:40)
    - Elihu's Speeches (32:1–37:24)
    - The Lord Speaks and Job Responds (38:1–42:9)
    - God Restores Job (42:10–17)

Five Top Sights and Spectacles of Job

Job Loses Everything (1:13–2:10) Watch as Job loses his possessions, his children, and finally his health.

Job's Useless Friends (3:1–26:14) Listen to Job's friends make accusations, and see how Job responds.

Job's Confession: My Redeemer Lives (19:23–27) Witness Job's great confession of faith in the resurrection of the Savior and in his own resurrection on the Last Day.

The Lord Challenges Job (38:1–40:2; 40:6–41:34) Hear the Lord remind Job that he cannot understand God's hidden will.

Job Confesses and God Restores (42:1–6, 10–17) Watch in awe as Job confesses his sin and God forgives him and completely restores him.

Seeing Jesus in Job

As New Testament believers, we have the advantage of knowing the work of Christ in fulfilling the Law through His life, death, and resurrection. Despite his suffering, Job believes in God's grace and mercy, which will be revealed in the coming Savior.

With Job, we can rejoice that one day we will see our Savior face to face.

For I know that my Redeemer lives,
and at the last He will stand upon the earth.
And after my skin has been thus destroyed,
yet in my flesh I shall see God,

whom I shall see for myself,
and my eyes shall behold, and not another.
My heart faints within me! (19:25–27)

Introduction and Satan's Challenge (1:1–2:13)

Job opens with a description of Job's prominence and wealth. When God speaks of Job's faithfulness, Satan challenges God to turn His hand against Job and see Job curse Him. God grants permission, and Satan afflicts Job. Job's three friends come to comfort him.

Job's Character and Wealth (1:1–5)

A man named Job from the land of Uz is greatly blessed. Job has ten children, a vast amount of livestock, and overall great wealth. Whenever Job's children have held a feast, Job has offered sacrifices in case his children had somehow committed sins.

From the text, what impression do you get of the effect Job's great wealth and prosperity had on him as a person? Is there enough here to tell if he was arrogant and selfish or humble and generous? (*Hint:* We'll get a lot more information in chapter 29.) In what ways do your financial situation and the way you use the gifts God has given you define you? your relationship with God? your relationship with other people?

CLEAR THE CONFUSION

How Did People View Wealth in Biblical Times?

In modern society, the attitude toward people who are extremely wealthy varies from great respect to contempt. In Bible times, many important leaders were blessed with great prosperity. Abraham, Isaac, and Jacob were all wealthy men. David and Solomon enjoyed great wealth and prosperity. Like each of these, Job was generous with the wealth God gave him and did not hoard it for himself.

Unfortunately, for many of God's people, as would prove true for Job's friends, the wealth of influential believers came to be considered the greatest measure of God's favor toward any specific person. If someone was wealthy, it was assumed that God was well pleased with that person. If someone suffered poverty, then he was assumed to be a sinner suffering the consequence of his sins.

Jesus attacked this false understanding quite often in His teachings. Perhaps the greatest example is His story of the rich man and Lazarus (Luke 16:19–31). Jesus described the incredible wealth of the rich man and the luxury he indulged in each day, then contrasted him with the poor beggar Lazarus, who sat at his gate desiring to be fed with the crumbs that fell from the rich man's table but did not receive anything from the rich man. The rich man died and received a lavish burial, while Lazarus died without even mention of a burial. For the crowd listening, the conclusion was clear: the rich man was a good man favored by God, while Lazarus must have been a horrible sinner to live such a horrible life.

Then Jesus turned the people's thinking on its head. Lazarus was carried by the angels to the most honored place in paradise, the bosom of Abraham, while the rich man was tormented in Hades. Job's friends would soon wrongly judge his integrity and his relationship with God based only on his fall from wealth, health, and prosperity. One of the important lessons of the book of Job is not to judge others or even your own standing with God merely on the circumstances in your life. We only stand in a good relationship with God through the merits of Jesus Christ, our Savior—nothing else.

Satan Allowed to Test Job (1:6–12)

Satan appears at a gathering of the sons of God. When God points out His faithful servant Job, Satan questions Job's loyalty, claiming that Job only remains faithful because God has blessed him with material prosperity.

In response, God allows Satan to test Job's loyalty and faithfulness. Satan may strike Job's possessions, but he may not afflict Job's body.

Satan Takes Job's Property and Children (1:13–22)

In the course of one day, Job experiences the loss of all he had and loved. The first messenger reports the theft of Job's oxen and donkeys along with the slaughter of his servants who tended them. The second messenger reports how fire from heaven (most likely lightning) had consumed the sheep and the servants attending them. The third messenger explains how the Chaldeans had captured all of Job's camels.

The final messenger brings the worst news of all. Job's sons and daughters had all been gathered together in one place when a windstorm destroyed the house, killing all of Job's children.

Upon hearing of this final disaster, Job tears his robe in shock, shaves his hair in immense grief, and falls to the ground in humble worship. He reveals amazing trust in God as he says, "Naked I came from my mother's womb, and naked shall I return. The Lord gave, and the Lord has taken away" (v. 21). Even with such intense grief and loss, Job does not blame God or sin against Him.

?

How does Job show he was invested in his children's lives and felt their loss deeply? How can fear of loss keep us from investing in the lives of our loved ones and the people God places in our lives?

SET THE SCENE

What was this gathering of the sons of God?

The Scriptures use the term *sons of God* to describe God's angels, part of His created order. The text does not explain why the angels were gathered before God, merely that they had done so. Satan had been among the angels before his rebellion and seems at this time to have had access to God's throne room.

When God asked Satan where he had come from, Satan replied that he had come from wandering on the earth. This reinforces Peter's warning to "be sober-minded; be watchful. Your adversary the devil prowls around like a roaring lion, seeking someone to devour" (1 Peter 5:8). It seems Satan's sole purpose is to search out the faithful and lead them into sin and hopelessness—to draw them away from fearing, loving, and trusting their merciful God.

Satan Attacks Job's Health (2:1–10)

After these events, Satan appears again at the gathering of the sons of God. When God questions his appearance, Satan repeats his statement about wandering upon the earth. When God again commends Job's faithfulness, Satan accuses Job of remaining faithful only because he still has his health. God allows Satan to afflict Job's health but does not permit him to take Job's life.

PICTURE OF THE SAVIOR

The Suffering Servant

Throughout the book of Job, we read of Job's intense physical and emotional suffering, from the loss of his children and possessions to the outbreak of sores on every part of his body. Job humbled himself as he sat in ashes, scraping his sores with a bit of broken pottery.

The image of Job as God's suffering servant foreshadows the life and work of Jesus Christ as our Suffering Servant. In addition to the physical pain of His flogging and crucifixion, Christ suffered the weight of sin for the entire world.

> Have this mind among yourselves, which is yours in Christ Jesus, who, though He was in the form of God, did not count equality with

> God a thing to be grasped, but emptied Himself, by taking the form of a servant, being born in the likeness of men. And being found in human form, He humbled Himself by becoming obedient to the point of death, even death on a cross. (Philippians 2:5–8)

LINK BETWEEN THE TESTAMENTS

Satan Tests Job → The Temptation of Jesus (Job 1:6–2:10 → Matthew 4:1–11)

God permitted Satan to test a faithful man, Job, with all kinds of hardship: poverty, death of loved ones, and serious physical illness. In a very similar manner, Jesus underwent a series of trials from Satan at the very beginning of His ministry. While the precise manner of Satan's temptations may have been polar opposites of one another, both reveal the single trick Satan uses to draw us away from God. Satan deprived comfortable Job of blessings yet offered many wondrous things to Jesus, who was weary and battered. God reveals that Satan seeks to inflate our egos so we prize ourselves above the God who loves us dearly.

Furthermore, both accounts help us to recognize the best defense against spiritual onslaught: our trust in and the faithful application of God's Word. Jesus soundly trounced every one of Satan's fantastical claims because He met them with the unfailing might of Scripture, which "is living and active, sharper than any two-edged sword" (Hebrews 4:12). While Job couldn't overcome his despair and questioning on his own, his submission to God and his faith in God's Word alone, no matter his present circumstances, proved extremely devastating to Satan's schemes. In these excellent case studies, God has given us powerful examples of how we can respond to the enemy's nastiest tactics.

Job's Three Friends (2:11–13)

Think about your closest friends. Whom would you want at your side if you were facing trauma and grief?

Job's three friends come to show him sympathy and comfort. Eliphaz the Temanite, Bildad the Shuhite, and Zophar the Naamathite will continue to appear throughout the book of Job. The friends hardly recognize Job in his condition. The friends spend seven days just sitting with Job in silence.

VISUALIZE

SET THE SCENE

Who were Job's friends? Why did they have such incorrect ideas about God?

Eliphaz the Temanite was a descendant of Esau, the brother of Jacob. These descendants were considered Edomites. Edom led many invasions against Israel. Bildad the Shuhite likely descended from Abraham through a concubine.

His tribe, the Midianites, were nomads. Little is known about Zophar the Naamathite, who is only mentioned here in Job.

Based on these various backgrounds, it is unlikely that Job's three friends would have had a strong knowledge of the true God, which would explain their false concepts of who God really is.

CLEAR THE CONFUSION

Was seven days of silence an appropriate way for Job's friends to react? Or was their presence more of a burden for Job?

The reaction of Job's friends was absolutely right and appropriate. They barely recognized him and sat with him in stunned silence. The fact that they stayed with him an entire week showed their genuine love and concern. Their silence acknowledged what a great loss Job had suffered.

?

What do you say to someone who has suffered a devastating loss? If you tend to avoid suffering or grieving people because you feel like you should say something but don't know what to say, what can you learn from Job's friends?

Dialogues Between Job and His Friends (3:1–26:14)

Three rounds of discussions take place between Job and his three friends. Each of Job's friends calls on him to turn from sin, while Job insists he has not done anything to cause God to afflict him with these disasters and suffering.

Job Laments His Birth (3:1–26)

After seven days of sitting in silence with his three friends, Job finally speaks. His misery causes him to lament the very day he was born. His lament includes not only a desire never to have been born but also a wish that he had died at birth or was even stillborn. Nothing gives Job comfort; he is filled with dread.

CLEAR THE CONFUSION

How could faithful Job experience such despair?

Many individuals falsely believe that people of faith somehow don't experience times of depression and despair. Faithful people who themselves experience despair or depression might even feel guilty for experiencing these emotions. Job's despair was great; he had already lost almost everything, and now he had lost his health.

When faced with the overwhelming weight of humanity's sin, our Lord experienced tremendous grief at the cost He faced on the cross. We see Jesus' deep sorrow and turmoil when He prayed on the Mount of Olives the night before His crucifixion.

> And He withdrew from them about a stone's throw, and knelt down and prayed, saying, "Father, if You are willing, remove this cup from Me. Nevertheless, not My will, but Yours, be done." And there appeared to Him an angel from heaven, strengthening Him. And being in agony He prayed more earnestly; and His sweat became like great drops of blood falling down to the ground. (Luke 22:41–44)

While in His deep despair, Jesus did not sin; instead, He turned to the Father in prayer. While Job lamented the day of his birth, he stopped short of blaming God for his despair.

Eliphaz Speaks: The Innocent Prosper (4:1–5:27)

Eliphaz decides he needs to reply to Job's lament. He begins his message by chiding Job for his impatience with God. Eliphaz reminds Job that while the innocent may experience suffering, they are never completely crushed by God. Only the unrighteous will experience God's final judgment.

Eliphaz understands that no one can be righteous before God. Even the angels are judged by God. Those who are foolish cannot please God; even the wise can be caught up in their own wisdom. Those who trust in the Lord will receive His blessings.

CLEAR THE CONFUSION

Why did Eliphaz say such meaningless things?

Eliphaz's speech was filled with generalities and vague promises. While well-intentioned, Eliphaz lacked a true understanding of the causes of suffering in this world. Eliphaz reduced the life of a believer to a series of behaviors and consequences. He saw God as the great judge, who dispenses blessings and punishment based only on man's behavior. He did not take into account suffering that is a result of living in a world ruined by sin or the results of another's sin or even the suffering that comes when a believer serves God faithfully.

Only when Eliphaz came to the concluding words of his speech did he begin to demonstrate a glimmer of understanding about how God truly deals with His faithful people. We are broken by sin, deserving only God's wrath and punishment. Yet in His mercy, God sent His Son to pay the price of our sin and give us His own righteousness.

Why do we so often feel the need to justify our actions before others? How can we avoid this sinful behavior?

Job Replies: My Complaint Is Just (6:1–30)

Job's response to his friend Eliphaz reflects his frustration with the lack of support Job feels from his friend. Instead of feeling comforted by Eliphaz, Job feels as if he is the target of God's poison arrows. He calls out to God like a hungry beast whose master has not provided feed. Job would be happy to die rather than face this misery.

Job says withholding kindness from a friend literally forsakes the love of God. Job does not ask his friends for money or even to rescue him from his situation. If nothing else, Job wishes his friends would just show him some empathy.

SET THE SCENE

What is Sheol?

The term *Sheol* appears sixty-five times in the Hebrew Old Testament. The exact meaning of *sheol* can vary depending on the context of its use:

1. The resting place of a person's mortal remains (see Job 17:16; Isaiah 38:10)
2. The place where both the righteous and unrighteous go when they die (see Genesis 37:35; Job 7:9; Psalm 16:10; 31:17; 89:48)
3. The place where God's judgment comes upon evildoers; the place God sends those who oppose Him (see Numbers 16:30, 33; Proverbs 5:5; Deuteronomy 32:22)

What images does Job use to express his suffering and the hopelessness he feels? What are some images people would understand today?

Job Continues: My Life Has No Hope (7:1–21)

Job compares his time on earth to hard labor, even slavery, which many experience. He desires for his time of service to be completed. Life passes as quickly as a weaver's shuttle. Job desires for his life and suffering to pass on quickly since he sees no hope for the future.

VISUALIZE

Looms and Shuttles

Job references a device common to people in that day to express how rapidly life passes. Ancient looms consisted of a large wooden frame with a series of parallel vertical threads called the *warp*. The shuttle, containing the weft thread, was passed between alternating warp threads to form the pattern as the fabric was formed. The shuttle moved back and forth at a rapid and constant rate, adding a single thread at each pass. An experienced weaver could pass the shuttle so quickly she could create up to thirteen yards of fabric a day. Job's reference to the weaver's rapidly moving shuttle reflects the swiftly passing years of life.

Bildad Speaks: Job Should Repent (8:1–22)

Bildad steps up with a message for his friend Job. But this message is far from the empathy Job is looking for. Instead, Bildad calls Job's words a "great wind" (v. 2). Bildad goes on to accuse Job of sinfulness; otherwise, God would come to Job's rescue. All Job needs to do is repent, and God will restore him.

Job Replies: There Is No Arbiter (9:1–35)

Job begins his proclamation: "Truly I know that it is so: But how can a man be in the right before God?" (v. 2). He acknowledges his unworthiness to stand before the righteous God and demand anything, for this same God created the very sun, moon, and stars.

God's anger at our sin is justified. When we claim to be blameless, we only condemn ourselves. Job realizes how quickly life is passing. Job believes that there is no arbiter between himself and God; he cannot possibly stand before God.

?

Job feels like God is far, far away. Why does Job wish he had an arbiter to stand between God and him? When you think of Jesus as our arbiter, what do you imagine Him saying to God the Father while Job was suffering? What do you imagine He says when you are going through very painful times?

SET THE SCENE

What is an arbiter?

Arbiters have the ultimate authority to settle disputes or disagreements between two individuals or between two groups. Arbiters include judges or other government authorities. Sports umpires and referees might also be considered arbiters in our world today. Jesus is the ultimate arbiter between God and mankind.

Job Continues: A Plea to God (10:1–22)

Job cries out to God as he attempts to understand why God has chosen him for such suffering. How does God view His people? Does He search out the sinner for punishment? Job tries to understand the mind of God as he pleads to God for mercy.

Zophar Speaks: You Deserve Worse (11:1–20)

Now Job's third friend, Zophar, takes his turn responding to Job's plea to God for mercy. However, Zophar's response is far from the support Job desires from his friends. Instead, Zophar contends that Job actually deserves far worse for asserting his righteousness before God.

CLEAR THE CONFUSION

How could Job's friends be so negative?

For those who live under God's grace, fulfilled in the life and work of Jesus Christ, it can be difficult to understand the negativity of Job's three friends. As Christians, we experience the Gospel in our daily lives as we repent and receive forgiveness from God for our sins. The practice of Confession and Absolution is at the very heart of our weekly worship life.

The same cannot be said for Job's three friends. In their minds, a person earned favor with God by good works and earned disfavor by evil works. Thus, they believed the state of a person's life showed where he stood with God. As long as Job prospered, God was rewarding the good life he was living. But with all Job's loss and suffering, God was showing His displeasure, so Job's friends concluded Job must have committed some great sin. The greater the suffering, the greater the sin that caused it—theirs was a theology of glory.

We see this same thinking in play in the Gospels when Jesus' disciples came upon a man born blind and asked Him, "Rabbi, who sinned, this man or his parents, that he was born blind?" (John 9:2). Jesus' answer stunned them: "It was not that this man sinned, or his parents, but that the works of God might be displayed in him" (John 9:3).

This same theology of glory turned the Jewish crowds against Jesus when they saw Him hanging on the cross. They thought God would never do such a shameful thing to the true Messiah, so they concluded Jesus of Nazareth was clearly a fraud and that God was displaying that by having Him crucified for His blasphemy.

But Jesus' suffering was the theology of the cross. Sometimes God permits His beloved children to suffer—not in punishment for their sin but to drive them to find comfort and strength in Him. Then we will be prepared to comfort others in their suffering (see 2 Corinthians 1:3–5). We live under God's grace, knowing the promise of salvation that is ours through the life, death, and resurrection of Jesus Christ. This allows us to live life with a positive attitude even when suffering tremendous pain or grief. We know the hope that is ours in Christ: the hope that just as Jesus entered into His glory when the Father vindicated Him by raising Him from the dead, so we will also be vindicated by God the Father when Christ returns and brings us into His kingdom of glory.

?

Why can't the theology of glory bring any lasting comfort and hope to people who are suffering or grieving? Why is the theology of the cross, Jesus' cross and empty tomb, able to give that comfort and hope?

Job Replies: The LORD Has Done This (12:1–25)

Job begins his response to his friends with a tone of sarcasm, addressing Eliphaz, Bildad, and Zophar as the people with whom "wisdom will die" (v. 2). Job realizes his friends think more highly of themselves than they deserve because they aren't suffering as Job is. Even the wild beasts have more wisdom than these three men. All mankind depends on the direction given by God.

Job Continues: Still I Will Hope in God (13:1–28)

Job continues to confront his friends and their lack of understanding of the work and care of God. They claim to speak for God, but all they speak is falsehoods. Job's only wish is that God will not hide or turn Himself from Job.

CLEAR THE CONFUSION

How could Job take his flesh in his teeth?

Job's statement "Why should I take my flesh in my teeth?" (v. 14) only appears once in the entirety of the Scriptures. Biblical scholars believe this figure of speech implies that Job was in so much grief and pain that he wanted to bite his own flesh to keep from crying out or complaining. A modern-day equivalent might be the expression "to bite your tongue" in order to keep from speaking out of turn.

Job Continues: Death Comes Soon to All (14:1–22)

Job uses the image of a lake or river that dries up completely to describe death. What experiences in your life have made you feel the reality of death and the fact that there is no returning to this present world after death?

Throughout time, mankind has struggled with the reality of our own mortality. Job ponders this reality, using a number of images tied to his own life experiences, especially his current situation. Job hints at the reality of his own resurrection: "Oh that You would hide me in Sheol [death], that You would conceal me until Your wrath be past, that You would appoint me a set time [day of resurrection], and remember me!" (v. 13). In chapter 19, we will see how Job more clearly expresses his hope.

LINK BETWEEN THE TESTAMENTS

Job Faces Death → The Resurrection on the Last Day (Job 14:10–17 → 1 Corinthians 15:52–53)

Job contemplated the reality of his existence and his impending death. He desired that God would cover over his sins and hide him away in death until the end of time, when God would raise His people and call them to Himself.

In his first letter to the church at Corinth, Paul painted a dramatic picture of Christ's second coming and the resurrection of the dead. Christ's sudden appearance and the sound of the trumpet will recall the faithful dead unto Himself.

Eliphaz Accuses: Job Does Not Fear God (15:1–35)

Beginning a second round of discussion, Job's friend Eliphaz begins his message by telling Job that he is full of wind. Eliphaz accuses Job of ignoring the wise counsel his friends are attempting to give him; he tells him the longer Job ignores their admonition to fear God, the worse things will become. In Eliphaz's viewpoint, Job thinks far too highly of himself and his status before an angry God.

Job Replies: Miserable Comforters Are You (16:1–22)

Job responds to his so-called friends and their lack of true comfort during his suffering. They have become men with lots of words for Job but little action. Job feels completely broken and abandoned by God even as he humbles himself before the Lord.

SET THE SCENE

How did Job continue to have hope for the future?

Despite the constant criticism from his friends and his seemingly hopeless situation, Job lived a life trusting in God's mercy. Job expressed this hope in chapter 16: "Even now, behold, my witness is in heaven, and He who testifies for me is on high . . . that He would argue the case of a man with God" (vv. 19, 21).

Note how this language hints at legal proceedings, with witnesses who testify on behalf of the accused and an intercessor who argues man's case before God, the righteous judge. This image of the legal proceedings before God continues in chapter 17: "Lay down a pledge for me with You; who is there who will put up security for me?" (v. 3). Job desired that God Himself would speak on his behalf.

As Christians, we know that Job's hope was fulfilled in the person of Jesus Christ, who serves as our advocate before the Father. Through His death and resurrection, Christ paid the price for our sins and takes our punishment upon Himself.

Job Continues: Where Then Is My Hope? (17:1–16)

Early in this chapter (v. 3), Job expresses his hope in his heavenly mediator. But suddenly the reality of his condition returns as he despairs for his life. Job desires nothing more than to lie in the peacefulness of his grave as he goes down to Sheol.

Bildad Speaks: God Punishes the Wicked (18:1–21)

Once again, Bildad expresses his legalistic viewpoint as he warns Job of the potential consequences of his sin. Bildad's message implies that he believes that Job's days on this earth are numbered and the wrathful God will soon bring judgment upon Job.

Job Replies: My Redeemer Lives (19:1–29)

WAYPOINT

What does this text show us?

The nineteenth chapter of Job reflects two distinct images. The chapter begins with Job expressing despair as he considers the dire condition of his life. Job has called out to God for mercy but has heard no answer. His physical

How can Job be so confident in the promise of the Messiah? How does Job's great confession give you confidence in God's promise?

The hymn "I Know That My Redeemer Lives" (*LSB* 461) uses the word *lives* in every one of the eight stanzas. Review the text of the hymn and note the various messages of reassurance found in each stanza.

Job's words in Job 19:25 inspired composer George Frideric Handel to write the aria "I Know That My Redeemer Liveth" as part of his masterpiece, *Messiah*. Video recordings of this inspirational piece can be found online.

health has declined to the point that death seems preferable to living with suffering. Job's friends and family have failed him and in fact "abhor" him (v. 19). Job describes his physical appearance with a disturbing image: "My bones stick to my skin" (v. 20).

Suddenly Job's perspective and tone change. Job desires that somehow his words would be recorded in a book for all to see. Job's words should be recorded for all time on stone: "For I know that my Redeemer lives" (v. 25). Job believes that one day he will see his Savior in the flesh, with his own eyes. The message shifts from despair to hope. And from this moment, Job does not sink as low in his grief and sorrow as before.

What does this text reveal about God's plan of salvation?

The most telling phrase in the entire book is Job's great confession, "I know that my Redeemer lives." With these words, Job declares his belief in the promise of the coming Savior. Evidently, Job knew the prophecies concerning the Messiah and His death and resurrection, and he confesses this confident hope here.

What does this text uncover about our identity and calling as God's people today?

Like Job, we can trust in God's promised Messiah in the person of Jesus Christ. As believers, we, too, will see our Savior face to face. Until that time, we can live in the promise of life eternal with our Creator.

PICTURE OF THE SAVIOR

Our Heavenly Mediator

As Job rhetorically wrestled with his friends about the nature of his suffering, he landed upon a moment of clarity that magnifies Jesus' character amid the chaos. Job recognized a few key truths about God through his evaluation of the disaster that had come upon him. First, he correctly identified that God is the utmost and highest judge there is, and because of this, nothing could pardon a man from God's Law except God Himself. Moreover, he discovered that in order to receive such a pardon, one must submit himself fully to God with the understanding that he cannot rescue himself in any way. The foundational concepts Job reckoned with point straight to Jesus Christ, the Second Person of the Trinity, who would come to justify mankind before His Father by His own blameless life, death, and resurrection. Only through faith in Him does anyone find pardon from the terminal, guilty condition of sin. And in this pardon, we can also find rest and comfort like Job, who boldly declared his confidence in his living Redeemer.

Zophar Speaks: The Wicked Will Suffer (20:1–29)

As Zophar speaks for a second time, he focuses on the calamities facing those who continue in their wicked ways. Zophar's message reflects his belief that somehow the righteous are exempt from suffering. The problem with this theology of glory is that no one is truly righteous before our perfect God: "For all have sinned and fall short of the glory of God" (Romans 3:23). The other problem with Zophar's theology is that sometimes God permits the wicked to prosper and believers to suffer.

?

Zophar's comments hurt Job deeply because Job knew they were completely untrue. Describe a time you or someone you know was suffering and heard something like this. Why is the suffering of Jesus on the cross much more comforting in those times of life?

Job Replies: The Wicked Do Prosper (21:1–34)

As Christians, we may relate to Job's message in chapter 21. In spite of the wicked things they do and their outright unbelief, sometimes unbelievers still experience lives filled with success and material prosperity. Because they have no concern for the afterlife, they enjoy what they have in this life and see death only as an end. This attitude of living life only for themselves results in their eternal damnation.

?

Why is it difficult to witness to an unbeliever who enjoys wealth, success, prosperity, or popularity?

LINK BETWEEN THE TESTAMENTS

Looking Beyond This Life → God's Comfort (Job 21:1–26 → 2 Corinthians 1:3–5)

In the midst of his discourse with foolish friends, Job argued an incredibly important point about the faithful life that remains timeless for all believers. Chapter 21 recounts Job's answer to the claim that God permits suffering exclusively to punish the wicked. His remarks pointed out that the world is chock full of wicked people who live pleasant lives and never experience the level of hardship he faced. It's a very effective rebuttal, but unfortunately, Job didn't carry this line of reasoning to its conclusion.

Not to worry, though, because the apostle Paul finished this thought when writing his second letter to the Corinthians:

> Blessed be the God and Father of our Lord Jesus Christ, the Father of mercies and God of all comfort, who comforts us in all our affliction,

> so that we may be able to comfort those who are in any affliction, with the comfort with which we ourselves are comforted by God. For as we share abundantly in Christ's sufferings, so through Christ we share abundantly in comfort too. (2 Corinthians 1:3–5)

Since we can't look to our earthly circumstances for comfort or assurance of God's love, then we must look to God and the promise fulfilled in Christ, concluded Paul. In this way, God's faithful people from the days of the patriarchs, the early church, and today have preserved this understanding and drawn confidence from the God of infinite comfort, who never fails His people.

Eliphaz Speaks: Job's Wickedness Is Great (22:1–30)

Eliphaz once again accuses Job of living only for himself. Eliphaz accuses Job of ignoring the needs of the poor and needy, thus displeasing God. He claims Job needs to listen to God and follow His guidance. He promises when man heeds the Lord's direction, he will be blessed.

Job Replies: Where Is God? (23:1–24:25)

Job laments, recounting the many ways God has hidden Himself. Despite Job's repeated searching—in every possible direction—God continues to elude Job. Job counters the theology-of-glory claims by recounting the suffering of the poor, who gather what little food they can find. In their poverty, they do without even basic essentials. Then there are others who rebel against the light of God. They perform evil deeds, causing pain and suffering for others. Despite their evil ways, their lives are extended and they seem to face no sufferings from God.

?

Describe a time in your life when you cried out to God but felt He was far away or hidden. What, if anything, helped you overcome that feeling?

LINK BETWEEN THE TESTAMENTS

Where Is God? → Eyes of Faith (Job 23:1–24:25 → Hebrews 11)

Job presented another powerful facet of faith shortly after his precursor (in chapter 21) to the Pauline encouragement. Job confessed that even while he might have been unable to find or see God, he understood that God's will is unchanging. True, this admission may have been marred by his disdain for God's incomprehensible will for him. Nevertheless, it is an important feature of Job's faith, which the author of Hebrews identified in other biblical examples, such as Noah's journey with the flood:

> And without faith it is impossible to please Him, for whoever would draw near to God must believe that He exists and that He rewards

> those who seek Him. By faith Noah, being warned by God concerning events as yet unseen, in reverent fear constructed an ark for the saving of his household. By this he condemned the world and became an heir of the righteousness that comes by faith. (Hebrews 11:6–7)

Job's "eyes of faith" helped him focus on God's consistent character instead of the unpleasant circumstances in which he suffered, just as the greatest heroes of faith would do in God's great plan of salvation through Jesus Christ.

Bildad Speaks: Man Cannot Be Righteous (25:1–6)

In the final speech of the three friends, Bildad asserts that man is incapable of righteousness. Man is born of sinful woman. Bildad refers to man as "a maggot" and the son of man as "a worm" (v. 6). But his argument is very short. Zophar will have nothing to add. None of them are able to convince Job that they are correct.

Job Replies: God's Majesty Is Unsearchable (26:1–14)

Job recounts the wonder of God's majestic works. His words reflect the Almighty's power over all creation—everything and everyone in it. God's power extends over every part and detail of the universe He made. The chapter concludes with the message that all these wonders are but the mere "outskirts" or "whisper" of God's power and majesty (v. 14).

? Where do we see God's majesty on display in the world today?

Job's Monologues (27:1–31:40)

Having silenced his three friends, Job presents his summary defense and begs for an opportunity to speak with God and present his defense to the Almighty.

Job Continues: I Will Maintain My Integrity (27:1–23)

Job recommits himself to maintaining his truthfulness before God. He will hold fast to his righteousness before the Lord for the rest of his life. Job prays that God would carry out justice on his enemies. Job warns that the unjust face the potential of sudden terror, as their fortunes could be swept away at any moment.

LINK BETWEEN THE TESTAMENTS

Hope in the Face of Doubt → Endurance and Hope (Job 27 → Romans 5:1–11)

Despite the doubts fueled by his physical and emotional condition, Job remained faithful to his Savior. We see this expressed in Job 19:25, "For I know that my Redeemer lives," but the theme of trust and hope in the face of doubt repeats throughout the book of Job. In Job 27, he expressed a sincere doubt that God was even listening to his cries for help. Yet Job vowed to remain faithful to God despite the nagging doubts concerning God's perceived inattentiveness.

In his letter to the Romans, Paul addressed these same issues of suffering and hope: "We rejoice in our sufferings, knowing that suffering produces endurance, and endurance produces character, and character produces hope" (Romans 5:3–4). The reason for Paul's hope becomes apparent as you continue to read Romans 5. Paul's faith was firmly anchored in the reality of Christ's death and resurrection. At times, we may feel Job's overwhelming sense of abandonment, yet we have hope in the promise of salvation through the saving work of Jesus Christ.

How does our world confuse wisdom with being smart? What is the difference between the two?

Job Continues: Where Is Wisdom? (28:1–28)

Mankind searches for wealth in all kinds of places. Their desire for gold, silver, and precious stones leads them to hidden-away places. Yet all this wealth cannot begin to compare to true wisdom. All the precious gems of the earth will not buy the wisdom of God.

Only God knows true wisdom; He alone serves as the source of all wisdom in all the world, since He alone created all wisdom. "Behold, the fear of the Lord, that is wisdom, and to turn away from evil is understanding" (v. 28).

SET THE SCENE

Wisdom in God's Word

Job made it very clear that the only true source of wisdom is found in God, who created and completed all things. Job's speech in chapter 28 set the stage for all God's wisdom that follows—both in the book bearing Job's name and in all the others that follow.

The Bible's five Books of Wisdom are not theoretical or speculative; rather, they offer real, practical wisdom. Rooted and established by God, this wisdom exceeds any man-made wisdom.

Job's Summary Defense (29:1–30:31)

Job's summary of his life in these two chapters takes two very distinct looks at Job's life experience. Chapter 29 recounts Job's life before God had allowed Satan to test him. Job longs for the days of old, when he felt God was watching over him and keeping him constantly in His care. When Job walked through the city, everyone gave him honor and respect. Men waited on his counsel and sat in silence as Job shared his advice.

Chapter 30 shifts gears to Job's life following his losses. Gone is the honor he once received. The children of the men Job once raised up and provided for now laugh at him and share the horrors of Job's life with one another. They all ignore Job's cries for help.

Job's Final Appeal (31:1–40)

Job makes one final appeal concerning his innocence before God and his friends. Each section of the chapter begins with some version of Job's assertion "If I have . . ." and the consequence he should face. But Job genuinely feels he has not been guilty of any of these intentional offenses against the Lord. The chapter concludes, "The words of Job are ended" (v. 40).

CLEAR THE CONFUSION

How did Job fall into a false understanding of works-righteousness?

Throughout the book of Job, Bildad, Eliphaz, and Zophar reflected their bias toward works-righteousness. So it should come as no surprise that Job himself began to believe that somehow he could earn God's favor through his actions.

As sinful human beings, we fall into the trap of thinking we somehow deserve God's love and mercy because of the good things we have done. But the truth is we are all sinful and deserve nothing but God's condemnation. "For all have sinned and fall short of the glory of God" (Romans 3:23). But the good news is that God's message doesn't end there: "And are justified by His grace as a gift, through the redemption that is in Christ Jesus" (Romans 3:24). Through Christ's death and resurrection, we receive the blessing of forgiveness and eternal life with Him.

Elihu's Speeches (32:1–37:24)

When Job and his three friends are finished speaking, a young man named Elihu speaks up to defend the honor of the Lord and call upon Job to repent and trust in God.

If you are a young Christian, or you remember being young, recall a time when you disagreed with an older Christian but felt the need to listen quietly. If you are older, what advice would you give young Christians afraid to speak up in the presence of their elders?

Elihu Rebukes Job's Three Friends (32:1–22)

The book of Job takes a sudden turn with the appearance of a new character—Elihu. Elihu is a young man who has shown his respect by silently listening to the discussion between Job and his three friends. Noticing all four men have had their say and that Bildad, Eliphaz, and Zophar have been unable to convince Job of his errors, Elihu declares that he must speak up.

Elihu's words reflect his disappointment in the three friends and their lack of helpful messages for their friend Job.

PICTURE OF THE SAVIOR

Elihu

Even after Job had made critical, true revelations about God, he succumbed to the belief that God was unjust to lay these sufferings upon him. Elihu, a young outsider, waited until Job and his friends had said their piece, and then he interjected in defense of God's justice. He rejected Job's haughty view of himself and affirmed that God doesn't bring suffering simply to punish the wicked but also to deliver and open the eyes of His people to His majesty. By properly recognizing God's character as He revealed Himself and by teaching others about Him, Elihu reflected a snippet of the coming Christ's ministry on earth.

Like Elihu, Jesus was a young man (early thirties) who respectfully corrected older priests, scribes, Pharisees, and rabbis who were misleading others with bad teaching. Jesus sought first to glorify His heavenly Father by showing others God's love for them. The climax of this mission came when He took upon Himself the ultimate suffering to deliver all people from their sins and the punishment of death.

Job's biggest mistake was trying so hard to justify himself to his friends that he ended up accusing God of being unjust. How important do you find it is for you to justify your actions and decisions to others? When is it better to humble ourselves and let others misjudge us, knowing that God knows the truth and will vindicate us at the right time?

Elihu Rebukes Job (33:1–33)

Having chastised Job's three friends, Elihu now turns to Job himself. Elihu calls Job to task for proclaiming his self-worthiness and reminds Job that no one is righteous before God. Elihu reminds Job to remain silent before God and listen to his advice.

Elihu Asserts God's Justice (34:1–37)

Elihu encourages those listening to give heed to his words. Though Job may claim his righteousness, God is the only one who is truly just. He shows no favoritism, treating both the noble and ordinary the same. God sees everything we say and do. Job speaks and acts against God without wise judgment.

Elihu Condemns Job (35:1–16)

Mankind has no right to consider ourselves sinless before God. We cry out to God for mercy and await His justice. Despite Job's many words of complaint before God, it is the Lord alone who chooses to remove our transgressions.

CLEAR THE CONFUSION

Is lamenting a sign of unbelief?

We live in an era of the positive. *Prosperity* and *positivity* are the buzzwords of business, personal life, and spirituality in the world today. The very idea of focusing on lamenting in sorrow seems contrary to the teaching of faith and life. Yet sometimes believers find themselves lamenting the situations in their lives. While lamenting can reflect our lack of faith and trust at times, it is not necessarily sinful or an indication of unbelief.

An entire book in our Bible is named Lamentations because it bemoans the desolate situation in Jerusalem after the city was conquered by the Babylonians and its people carried off into exile. The book of Psalms contains psalms of lamentation. David wrote laments following the death of King Saul and his son Jonathan, David's dear friend. Even Jesus' cry from the cross is a lament: "My God, My God, why have You forsaken Me?" (Matthew 27:46).

Because we are living in a world ruined by sin and are suffering the consequences of those sins, lamentation is a godly way to pour out our souls before God and cry out for His comfort and peace. In fact, Martin Luther said that believers should certainly lament their sinfulness and repent of their sins before God, who graciously forgives for the sake of His Son, Jesus Christ. Lamenting is much healthier than trying to push our sorrows deep inside in an effort to never question God.

Elihu Extols God's Greatness (36:1–33)

WAYPOINT

Review chapter 36. What are some words or phrases used by Elihu that reflect God's greatness?

What does this text show us?

Elihu boldly speaks on behalf of our mighty God, whose eye is always on both the righteous and the sinner. God upholds those who call to Him but allows those who disregard His Word to face judgment.

We can look upon the work of the Lord in our lives and see His greatness. All mankind comes to Him for rescue and salvation. We cannot begin to understand God's work in our lives. He judges the people with justice and opens their eyes to His mighty power.

How could Elihu's message serve as a reassurance for Job concerning God's promise of salvation?

What does this text reveal about God's plan of salvation?

Elihu's perspective on suffering differs greatly from Job's viewpoint. Up to this point, Job verbally laments the seeming silence of the Lord as he experiences pain and loss. Job feels as if God remains silent despite his pleas for mercy and relief.

Elihu's perspective on Job's suffering focuses on how God acts in the life of a believer. Because God is perfectly wise and just, as well as infinitely compassionate, He uses suffering to accomplish His purpose. Sometimes that purpose is to remind the believer that he or she is not in control but rather totally dependent on God and His mercy. Suffering develops character and guides the faithful to realize the importance of discipline in the life of the believer.

How can we apply Elihu's message as Christians in the world today?

What does this text uncover about our identity and calling as God's people today?

Just as God allowed Job to be tested, so He calls His people to faithful living today. However, living in faith can be challenging in this sin-filled world. The life of a Christian involves beliefs and practices that stand in opposition to the rest of society. This can make everyday living difficult and motivate the believer to depend solely on the mercy and grace of the Savior.

Elihu Proclaims God's Majesty (37:1–24)

Elihu describes the might and power of God on display using dramatic images of thunder, lightning, and other natural phenomena. Elihu challenges Job to consider the work of God and how He created the earth and continuously cares for His creation. We must stand in awe of God and His mighty power.

The Lord Speaks and Job Responds (38:1–42:9)

Finally, Job receives his chance as God appears to question him and hear his answer.

The LORD Answers Job (38:1–40:2)

Suddenly Elihu is finished and a new, unexpected voice speaks with the briefest introduction. "Then the LORD answered Job out of the whirlwind" (38:1). Job, who had lamented God's seeming silence, who had proclaimed, "Oh, that I knew where I might find Him, that I might come even to His seat! I would lay my case before Him and fill my mouth with arguments" (23:3–4). Now Job gets the hearing he requested. But instead of Job questioning God, God questions Job. The Lord begins with a series of questions essentially challenging Job: "Who do you think you are?"

The challenges in chapter 38 center around God's question "Where were you when I laid the foundation of the earth?" (v. 4). Throughout His answer, God refers to various wonders in the creation as He reminds Job that He is the Creator of them all. Job is merely a part of that created order and therefore has no right to question God concerning the Lord's oversight of His creation.

In chapter 39, the focus shifts from the creation itself to the variety of creatures made by God. Using the examples of mountain goats, wild donkeys, oxen, ostriches, horses, and hawks, God points out the futility of mankind trying to force God to conform to our will. Only He is in control, and He does as He pleases.

?

When Job spoke in earlier chapters, he forgot his place as a limited creature and spoke of things he didn't know, accusing God of things that were untrue and unfair. How much do you find yourself trying to understand what God is doing in every situation? Why is it wiser to confess our ignorance and humbly trust God our Creator and Savior to handle every situation? How can our prayers reflect that humility?

SET THE SCENE

Was God angry with Job? Why did He respond with such passion?

In this section of the Scriptures, we see God's righteous anger directed at Job for his lack of understanding and his faithlessness. Throughout the book, Job had questioned the Lord's care and seeming silence. God had tolerated the faithless speeches from Job's useless friends, but now the time had come for God to speak. The Lord's message asserted who He is and man's unworthiness to ask Him for anything.

Yet God would not leave Job with this admonition. As we read on through the rest of the book of Job, we see the gracious and merciful nature of our God. Like Job, we deserve nothing but God's wrath and judgment. Yet in His mercy, God sent His own Son, Jesus Christ, to pay the price for our sinful behavior. On the cross, God's righteous anger over sin fell upon Jesus instead of us. We receive His gift of forgiveness and life eternal with Him.

Job Promises Silence (40:3–5)

Job is struck silent by God's admonition. When God offers him a chance to answer (v. 2), Job pledges not to speak again but rather to listen for the Lord's direction.

LINK BETWEEN THE TESTAMENTS

God's Righteous Anger → Jesus Cleanses the Temple (Job 38–40 → Matthew 21:12–13)

The Lord's angry response to Job may come as a surprise to some readers who normally associate God's anger being directed only at His enemies, not the faithful. Yet God's anger with Job is certainly justified as Job falsely accused God of ignoring his plea for mercy. We see God's righteous anger at Moses in Exodus 4:24–26, when Moses failed to circumcise his sons as God's law required.

We see another example of God's righteous anger when Jesus drove the money-changers and animal sellers out of the temple courts. These businessmen had been allowed to set up their stalls in the courts of the temple, but they were known for their less-than-honest business practices and sometimes outright corruption. In driving them out of the temple courts, Jesus reminds us that the true purpose for gathering is to worship and honor Him.

The LORD Challenges Job (40:6–41:34)

God exposes Job's powerlessness before Him by pointing to two fearsome creatures before which man is terrified and powerless.

What things in nature are outside of human control and make you feel tiny and powerless?

VISUALIZE

Behemoth and Leviathan

The Lord addressed Job using two examples of mighty beasts that struck fear into men of Job's time. Some scholars believe these were mythical creatures, but God described these animals in factual terms, including man's efforts to capture and tame them. It would be strange for God to use a creature that did not exist to instill true fear and reverence in Job toward his God and Creator.

The Behemoth was a mighty land creature, a herbivore, who was equally at home on land or in the water along the river's edge. Based on the description in Job 40, some scholars suggest Behemoth may describe a hippopotamus or sauropod dinosaur descended from the animals Noah brought onto the ark.

By contrast, Leviathan lived in the water full-time. Leviathan could not be captured or even remotely controlled. His skin was so tough that harpoons and spears were ineffective. The description of Leviathan's scales suggest a creature related to present-day reptiles, perhaps a crocodile, plesiosaur, or other armored dinosaur.

The name *Behemoth* can be literally translated from Hebrew as "animal" or "beast." The word form used here in Job is actually plural but uses singular verbs.

Artists have attempted to create images of the Behemoth and Leviathan based on the biblical descriptions. This engraving, taken from an old Bible, suggests creatures with fanciful features based on the descriptions in Job 40–41.

Job's Confession and Repentance (42:1–6)

Faced with convicting evidence from the Lord, Job humbles himself and acknowledges his sinfulness before God. Through his confession, Job places himself at the mercy of God as he pledges to repent and listen for the voice of the Lord.

How did Job's experience with God change his outlook? When you think of the challenges in your life and put yourself in Job's place standing before God, how do God's words transform your outlook on your life?

PICTURE OF THE SAVIOR

Job's Suffering Intercession

Upon hearing God's Word spoken against his faulty understanding, Job at last recognized who he was in relation to the almighty God he had scorned because of his suffering. He submitted to God in repentance and confessed his unworthiness in a public display, covering himself in dust and ashes as a sign of his worthlessness.

When God commanded Job to pray for his friends, who had sinned so grievously against him and increased his suffering, Job made a grand sacrifice on their behalf and prayed earnestly for them. Not only was this act of love an outward sign of his contrite heart, but it also pointed to the very Redeemer he had confessed in his debate with his friends. Job did not call judgment down upon them or accuse them harshly, but in his own suffering, he recognized their selfsame need for God's grace and pleaded with God for their deliverance as well. Jesus would come to be our greatest Priest, interceding personally on our behalf and suffering the even greater pains of all sin so that all who have faith in Him might be reunited with God forever.

The LORD Rebukes Job's Friends (42:7–9)

God convicts Eliphaz—and with him Job's other two friends—for not speaking rightly about Him as Job had done. The three are instructed to make a sacrifice before God through the leadership of Job, who will pray for their forgiveness. The sacrifice is made as directed, and God pardons the three of their sin.

CLEAR THE CONFUSION

Why would God say Job spoke rightly of Him when Job had accused God of being unjust?

God was speaking about the two different theologies underlying Job's conversation and those of his friends. Job spoke rightly of God because he argued the theology of the cross. His friends misrepresented God by professing their theology of glory. This false theology slanders and oppresses true believers in their suffering and comforts prosperous sinners who need to be confronted for their sins.

Much pain has been caused by Christians who see a suffering brother or sister and say, "If you only had more faith, God would heal your cancer" or "You must have done something horrible for God to punish you like that." May God deliver us from such evil thinking and damaging speech.

God Restores Job (42:10–17)

In grace, God heals repentant Job and restores his prosperity.

The LORD Restores Job's Fortunes (42:10–17)

Having endured his trials and honored God with his repentance, Job now sees complete restoration of his fortunes. Those who had once despised him now bring him coins and gold. His lost herds of sheep, camels, oxen, and donkeys now double in number, and he is blessed with seven sons and three daughters. Job lives a long and blessed life, seeing the birth of four generations of his offspring.

CLEAR THE CONFUSION

Why did Job receive a double portion of what he lost?

When God restored Job's fortunes, He did so with interest, literally doubling the number of the livestock lost during Job's trials by Satan. The restoration of principal plus an additional amount is seen in other places in the Scriptures. When Jesus called Zacchaeus down from the sycamore tree, Zacchaeus pledged to return fourfold the money he had wrongly taken from people—a generous excess—reflecting the overflowing grace of our Lord and Savior (see Luke 19:8).

And in case you wonder why God didn't double the number of children for Job and his wife, He did. They had ten new children on earth, and their first ten children awaited them in eternity. Now they rejoice in God's presence with all twenty of their sons and daughters, looking forward to the day when their Redeemer will stand upon the earth, and in their risen flesh, they will see Him for themselves, and their eyes shall behold Him and not another.

?

When God restored Job's fortunes, He vindicated Job's faith, showing his friends that Job had been right all along and that his sufferings were not caused by any grievous sin he had committed. When Jesus was mocked and ridiculed on the cross, God vindicated Him through the darkness (Matthew 27:45), the tearing of the temple curtain and the earthquake (Matthew 27:51), and most of all, Jesus' resurrection on the third day (Matthew 28). How have you been vindicated or seen someone else be vindicated after being falsely judged or misunderstood? If that vindication has not yet come, how does Job's story help you be patient as you wait?

VISUALIZE

PSALMS

Welcome to Psalms

The book of Psalms is a wholly unique and pivotal book in the Bible. The Hebrew word *psalm* can be translated as "song of praise" or as a song accompanied by stringed instruments. This book, then, is the songbook of God's Old and New Testament people. The 150 gathered and curated songs were written over the span of centuries, with the oldest perhaps being written by Moses and the newest being written in the time between the Old and New Testaments. This collection, compiled in five different sections, includes songs of all types, including hymns of praise, lament, repentance, and even cursing! God's people in the Bible knew many if not most of these psalms by heart and would have sung or meditated on them on their own, in their households, and in their community worship. Delve into this amazing book and discover the heritage of song, history, and prophecy presented in the legacy of the Psalms. You'll find a psalm to fit every situation in your life walking with the Lord.

What is one question you have about the book of Psalms as you prepare to study it?

Psalms at a Glance

- **Start:** The book begins with two opening psalms that provide not only an introduction to the book but also two critical themes: the roles of God's Word and of God's Anointed, the promised Messiah.
- **End:** The book concludes with a series of psalms often called the "hallelujah psalms," which teach us how to praise our God.
- **Theme:** Psalms is the book of prayer and praise for God's people. In its many songs, which cover the full breadth of human emotion and experience, God's people cling to our hope in His salvation.
- **Author and Date:** The book of Psalms has many authors. Individual psalms are often attributed to certain authors, though it is unclear to what extent each psalm is meant to be understood as written by that person or written in tribute to that person. The main authors attributed in the book of Psalms include David, Asaph, and the sons of Korah. Dates of writing could be as early as the time of Moses

How does the vast scope of time and authors included in the book of Psalms impact how you read it?

(1400s BC) for Psalm 90, but most were written between around 1000 BC (for David) and 500 BC (the time of the returned exiles).

- **Places Visited:** Jerusalem mostly, especially the temple and Mount Zion
- **Journey Time:** The 150 psalms can be read in their entirety in under five hours.
- **Outline:**
  - Book One, Mostly Personal Psalms of David (1–41)
  - Book Two, Mostly Psalms of David About the Kingdom (42–72)
  - Book Three, Mostly Nationalistic Psalms of Asaph and the Sons of Korah (73–89)
  - Book Four, Mostly Anonymous Psalms and Laments (90–106)
  - Book Five, Mostly Songs of Ascents and Praise (107–150)

Five Top Sights and Spectacles of Psalms

The Opening Psalms (1–2) Witness how God orients the worship life of His people around understanding God's Word and God's Anointed One.

The Lord Is My Shepherd (23) Marvel at how this ancient psalm has comforted God's people for thousands of years in times of sadness and uncertainty.

Sit at My Right Hand (110) In this most-quoted chapter of the Bible in the New Testament, listen as David prophesies about the coming Messiah.

Your Word Is a Lamp to My Feet (119) Meditate on the power of God's Word for granting wisdom in the lives of God's people.

Hallelujah Psalms (146–150) Rejoice with God's people for all time over God's gracious mercy toward us!

Seeing Jesus in Psalms

It only makes sense that the songbook of God's Old and New Testament people would point to Jesus, since Jesus said regarding all the Old Testament Scriptures, "You search the Scriptures because you think that in them you have eternal life; and it is they that bear witness about Me"

(John 5:39). Throughout the book, there are both explicit prophecies about the coming Christ and implied nods to who He is and what He does. One of the key themes of the book is the role of God's anointed—usually meaning the king (often David). Yet when the psalms speak of the anointed king, they usually also imply or refer to the greater Anointed One to come, the Christ. Psalm 2 speaks of the role of the anointed as God's representative on earth, and in Psalm 110, David explicitly points to his Lord, the greater Anointed One, the Christ. In fact, the biblical themes of sin, repentance, forgiveness, and restoration through God's anointed (or Anointed One) are so prevalent throughout the book that Martin Luther referred to the Psalms as the "Little Bible." As you read through all the psalms, with their connections to both human life and the role of God in forgiving and restoring His people, rejoice in Jesus, the ultimate fulfillment of God's plan of salvation.

Book One, Mostly Personal Psalms of David (Psalms 1–41)

The book of Psalms, from ancient days, has been divided up into five collections, called *books*. The exact reason for these divisions is not included in the text, and it is thought that these divisions into books happened during the intertestamental time (between the writing of Malachi in 430 BC and the birth of Christ). This first collection of psalms is entirely comprised of personal psalms, most of which are directly attributed to David.

The Way of the Righteous and the Wicked (Psalm 1)

Psalms 1 and 2 serve as a dual introduction to the book of Psalms. Psalm 1 establishes the way of righteousness and wickedness. Wicked sinners will receive judgment and eternal punishment from God, while the righteous are established by God's Word. It is God's Word, which ultimately put on flesh in Jesus, that gives us forgiveness, life, and salvation.

?

If you had to rephrase the main theme of the first psalm in your own words, what would it be? Why would you phrase it that way?

LINK BETWEEN THE TESTAMENTS

God Judges the Wicked → The Final Judgment (Psalm 1 → Matthew 25:31–46)

Many of the psalms deal with the topic of wisdom in the form of following righteousness and shunning wickedness. The very fact that the first psalm introduces this theme shows the place that understanding godly wisdom has in the book. One thing is clear: God despises wickedness and loves righteousness. And we should too. In the New Testament, Jesus spoke of a final judgment for those who disobey God's Law. In light of this, we are guilty and deserve only God's judgment and wrath along with the wicked. Thanks be to God that we have the blessing of Jesus Christ, who died on the cross to forgive our sins. We who believe in Him are forgiven our sins and will not suffer the final judgment for our wickedness. Until that final judgment, we, too, can strive to faithfully live out our Christian identity by living wisely as we serve our neighbor in our daily lives.

The Reign of the LORD's Anointed (Psalm 2)

Psalm 1 introduces readers to the ways of wickedness and righteousness, key themes of the Psalms. Psalm 2 introduces the second theme: the role of God's Anointed. Those who plot against the anointed kings God has chosen will suffer God's wrath. This psalm looks forward to Jesus Christ, the Anointed One, who will judge the whole world, bringing salvation from God's enemies and refuge for all who trust in Him, and condemning unbelievers to hell.

Save Me, O My God (Psalm 3)

David wrote this psalm during the time he fled for his life from his son Absalom, who was attempting to usurp David's throne (2 Samuel 15–18). Absalom stole the hearts of Israel and had the Israelite army at his control. Only the loyal followers of David stayed at his side. This psalm is both a cry to God for rescue from our enemies and a confident declaration that God shields us from our foes.

CLEAR THE CONFUSION

Are the inscriptions at the start of certain psalms part of God's inspired Word?

Beginning with Psalm 3, many psalms begin with an inscription that explains something about the psalm, the author, the occasion for which it was written, or a tune to which it should be sung. These are all part of God's inspired Word. In the inscription for Psalm 3, we learn that David wrote this psalm when he fled from his son Absalom. When we read of that account in 2 Samuel 15–18, we can understand the reason David was so distraught in the opening words of the psalm. But as he poured out his heart to God, we can see the Lord comforting him while he is praying, strengthening his faith and giving him confidence his God will deliver him.

CLEAR THE CONFUSION

How should we understand the words *foes* and *enemies* in the book of Psalms?

The psalmists, especially David, often prayed for God's wrath and judgment over enemies. As the anointed king of Israel, David—and other anointed leaders—was chosen by God to shepherd and guide the nation of Israel. Enemy tribes and nations surrounded the Promised Land, and war was a constant problem. Not only these outside enemies but also internal enemies, like Saul and later Absalom, plagued David with danger throughout his life. In light of God's plan of salvation, we need to be careful with how we interpret these enemies in contemporary terms.

In the Old Testament, God established a national home for His people Israel as they awaited the Messiah. In New Testament times, which include our time today, God's people are not given a specific geographic nation. Instead, God's people are part of the church, and this exists wherever believers gather. The enemies of God's people in these end times are not tribes or nations but the fallen powers of the devil, the world, and our sinful flesh. As such, when we consider the "enemies" in the book of Psalms, we should not think specifically about national or tribal conflicts but about the devil and those things under the devil's influence that constantly threaten and tempt God's people into unbelief. In this light, we can earnestly pray for God to deliver us from the devil, the world, and our own sinful nature as we await Christ's return.

Answer Me When I Call (Psalm 4)

In this psalm, King David cries out to God that his enemies are seeking to discredit and shame him. David then addresses his enemies, and all who will read the psalm, reminding us that God sets the godly apart from those who slander them. This is a great instruction for all people in godly living.

The inscription shows David's intention for the choirmaster, the leader of the Levite choir, to sing this psalm with stringed instruments, likely harps, accompanying it.

Lead Me in Your Righteousness (Psalm 5)

David's psalm asks God to lead us out of the sins of boasting and deceit, as these bring us to destruction. Instead, God's people are to rejoice in His name and accomplishments, as He is righteous.

CLEAR THE CONFUSION

What is meant by *righteousness* in the book of Psalms?

The psalmists use the word *righteousness* quite a bit in the book. The word means being in a right state with something. There are two ways we can understand the word *righteousness* in the Bible. The first is the righteousness—rightness before God—that only comes to us as a gift of grace. Because of our sin, we are not in a right relationship with God and cannot enter heaven. Yet through Christ's perfection (righteousness), we have been made right with God. This is the core of Christianity: we are justified (made right) with God by grace through faith in God's promise to redeem His people.

Though Abraham in the Old Testament did not yet see Jesus, Abraham believed in God's promise of the coming Messiah, and God made him righteous (Genesis 15:6). Throughout the Bible, God's people were made righteous by faith in His promises (Habakkuk 2:4). This promise is ultimately fulfilled in Christ. By faith in Him and what He did on the cross and empty tomb to forgive our sins, we are made righteous before God as well (Romans 3:21–22).

A second way we can understand righteousness is in our relationships with others in this world. Because God's people are made righteous before God by grace through faith, we, too, can seek to live in that right relationship. This is not for our salvation but as an extension of it. God has given us His Law, summarized in the Ten Commandments. The Law always accuses us of our sins; however, it not only accuses us but also leads us and guides us, as God's made-righteous people, into the way of right living in that relationship. Though we fail to live this perfectly, we still strive to do righteous acts and think righteous thoughts in line with God's Word. In so doing, not only will we better understand who God is and what our relationship with Him is like, but we will also be better able to love and serve our neighbor.

In Psalms, the word *righteousness* is often (but not always) used in this second sense. Understanding how to discern these two types of righteousness as we read the Bible is an important art. Here in Psalm 5:8–9, we are to understand the word in the second sense. David asked God to lead him

?

How will you work to faithfully discern the proper definition of *righteousness* as you come across the term in the book of Psalms?

in the way of rightness before Him so that he might lead a faithful life in the midst of so many attacks and temptations.

O LORD, Deliver My Life (Psalm 6)

The psalmist pleads with God for rescue from all forms of emotional and physical pain and distress. This torment is brought about by his sins. Yet he and all of God's children can be confident that God hears our pleas for deliverance. In Christ, God has forgiven us and brought about deliverance from the consequences of our sins.

CLEAR THE CONFUSION

What does *Sheminith* in the superscription mean?

This Hebrew word literally means "eighth." It may refer to a musical setting or to an eight-stringed instrument.

LINK BETWEEN THE TESTAMENTS

Lord, Deliver Me → Jesus Heals and Defeats Death (Psalm 6 → Luke 8:26–56)

When David spoke of the serious afflictions of his sin, he wasn't kidding around. Upon his growing realization that his sinful condition was bringing him anxiety, weariness, grief, and discontent, he quickly cried out to God for deliverance. Sounds pretty awful, right?

That's not the end of it. God clearly shows us sin's destruction strikes every generation. In the Gospel of Luke, Jesus encountered people dealing with the same consequences of sin hundreds of years after this psalm had been written. A man was filled with wrathful demons, a woman with an incurable bleeding condition sought Jesus for reprieve, and a local leader named Jairus lost his daughter to the clutches of death before Jesus raised her up.

Sin is no joke, and Jesus attested to this fact when He took all sin upon Himself on the cross as an atoning sacrifice for our sake. Our world is still ravaged and scarred by the consequences of sin today, but we can live in the joy of Jesus' complete victory, confident that we are no longer slaves under the influence of death but freed unto life everlasting with Him.

In You Do I Take Refuge (Psalm 7)

David wrote this psalm at the false accusations of an enemy named Cush. This man is not mentioned in either 1 Samuel or 1 Chronicles. But since he was from the tribe of Benjamin, he was likely an ally of King Saul, who sought to kill David.

David writes this psalm confident of his righteousness before God. God will judge the unrepentant wicked man, but He will establish those who trust in Him and in His righteousness.

CLEAR THE CONFUSION

What does *Shiggaion* in the superscription mean?

This is a term used only rarely in the Old Testament in connection with a psalm or song set to music. That makes it difficult to grasp its full meaning. Commentators think it could refer to a complaint or lament.

How Majestic Is Your Name (Psalm 8)

David's great psalm of praise thanks God for His many blessings. The whole of creation gives glory to God, yet God establishes His human creatures to have dominion over it.

?

What most stands out to you about your relationship to God in light of Psalm 8?

CLEAR THE CONFUSION

What does *Gittith* in the superscription mean?

We are not sure of the meaning of this term. It could be a musical instrument or a particular melody.

SET THE SCENE

Music in Biblical Times

As you read the psalms, you'll come across many different musical terms in the superscriptions (headings) of the psalms and in the psalms themselves. The psalms were likely chanted (often responsively) rather than sung like we think of modern singing. The meaning and use of the term *Selah*, which is untranslatable in English, likewise is unclear. The term possibly refers to the use of certain musical instruments, such as the harp, or signals some sort of break or refrain in the psalm. Many of the psalms include what appear to be tunes in the superscriptions as well, signaling the basic melody that the psalm was designed to fit. These melodies are lost to time.

The instruments used by God's people in worship are many and fascinating. Included in the psalms, in addition to choirs, were percussive instruments like bells, cymbals, tambourines, and clapping. Stringed instruments used to accompany the psalms included the harp, lute, and lyre; and wind instruments included the flute, pipes, and trumpets. Though these would not directly resemble contemporary instruments of similar names, one can imagine the sort of music this varied mix of band and choir could make to accompany the psalms. In addition, dance was often included as an extension of the use of music. Though we often speak the words of the psalms solemnly in our worship services today, the delivery of the psalms was much more varied as the official worship songs of God's people throughout the Scriptures.

I Will Recount Your Wonderful Deeds (Psalm 9)

Psalms 9 and 10 are often considered to comprise one psalm, composed later in David's life. In Psalm 9, David praises God's graciousness to His people and justice against the wicked nations and peoples who oppose Him. In verses 15–16, David observes a way the Lord often works against His people's enemies: by making the evildoers fall into the very trap they laid for the righteous.

There are several great examples of this in the Old Testament. In the book of Esther, Mordecai's enemy Haman has a huge gallows built on which he plans to hang Mordecai, but when the king learns of his plot, Haman is hanged upon his own gallows (see Esther 7:7–10). Daniel's enemies used a law they manipulated the king into issuing to force the king to cast Daniel into the lions' den. When God closed the lions' mouths, the king rescued Daniel and threw his accusers into the den, and the lions killed them all before they hit the ground (see Daniel 6:19–24). God not only knows the deadly plots of our enemies, but He also knows how to turn those plots against them.

Why Do You Hide Yourself? (Psalm 10)

Does it ever feel to you that God is far away or doesn't care about the struggles you face? David expresses that same feeling as he recounts how the powerful victimize the poor and convince themselves God will never call them to account.

David reassures us with a confident prayer that God will root out those who are wicked and who oppress the weak and poor. In light of Christ, we praise God that He has had compassion on those of us who are oppressed by the ancient enemies of sin, death, and the devil.

The LORD Is in His Holy Temple (Psalm 11)

In this psalm, David is facing great danger. His counselors are advising him to flee Jerusalem and run to the mountains for safety. He expresses his faith in God as his refuge. He reminds them and us that God watches the wicked and the righteous. God is righteous and loves righteousness. He will protect the faithful and punish the wicked with fire and scorching wind, a vivid picture of hell. But the righteous through faith will behold God's face, a reminder of eternal life with God.

The Faithful Have Vanished (Psalm 12)

How do evils in your life compare to the evils David expressed in Psalm 12?

David cries out for help in the face of lies and betrayal. Amid this despair, though, he is confident in God's promises to guard and keep His people forever. This He has accomplished for us in the cross of Christ.

LINK BETWEEN THE TESTAMENTS

"You will guard us from this generation forever" → "Truly, I say to you, this generation will not pass away until all these things take place" (Psalm 12:7 → Matthew 24:34)

David spoke of a generation of evildoers who made great boasts with their tongues; they believed they were masters of their own fate and forgot God is their judge. This passage helps us interpret a confusing promise Jesus made in Matthew, Mark, and Luke while predicting the events of the end times. He said, "This generation will not pass away until all these things take place."

Some think Jesus made a false prediction, because His generation passed away long ago. But Jesus was not talking about generation in the sense of His contemporaries who were born in the same decade—or even those alive while He walked the earth.

He was speaking of a generation as a division within humanity, all those who deny God and live in unbelief, just as David had done in this psalm. Clearly, David was not saying that all of his contemporaries uttered lies, because he differentiated that wicked generation from the poor who are plundered, the generation of believers. So we can see the entire human race as made up of two generations: the unbelievers and the believers.

Jesus used this sense of the word *generation* when He told us there would be unbelieving people up until the day He returns to the judge the world.

CLEAR THE CONFUSION

Why are so many of the psalms about the evils of the world?

It is easy to fall into the trap of thinking that the Christian life should only focus on trying to be happy all the time. Though we can and should focus on God's blessings, God's people can look at reality for what it is. We live in a world broken by sin and death. The Psalms capture the depth and breadth of human experience. We can call evil and suffering for what it is and call the devil, the world, and our sinful flesh our enemies.

These evils, which infect the world and corrupt the human experience, constantly tempt God's people to despair of and abandon their faith. Yet in the midst of these evils, we have the sure and firm promise of Christ. He has not abandoned us but instead has conquered these ancient enemies for us through the cross and empty tomb. In Him, we have complete deliverance from the evils of this world. This is ours both now by the forgiveness of sins through the means of grace and ultimately in the new creation. With the psalmist, we can lament and cry out against the evils of the world, while at the same time, we rejoice in God's salvation.

How Long, O LORD? (Psalm 13)

Crying out to God for deliverance, David wonders why it seems like God has forgotten him. As those who doubt God's promises gloat over him, David pleads to God. Yet even though David knows only pain and suffering and sees no evidence that things are getting better, he trusts in God's steadfast love and sings to the Lord a song of praise.

How have you experienced similar feelings as those David expresses in Psalm 13? What can you learn from his example as he transitions from lament to hope-filled praise throughout the course of this psalm?

The Fool Says, There Is No God (Psalm 14)

David introduces an idea in this psalm that Solomon will pick up frequently in the book of Proverbs. The fool says in his heart there is no God. When the Bible calls someone a fool, it is not speaking of someone who is mentally deficient or does things without thinking; rather, it is referring to someone whom the world might call wise and shrewd but who denies God's existence.

In this psalm, David reminds us to step back and consider the full sweep of our human life. All of our lives will end with us standing before God for eternal judgment. All those who deny God forfeit eternal life and will suffer eternal torment—fools indeed.

In the final verse, David expresses the hope and desire of all the Old Testament saints: that "salvation for Israel would come out of Zion"

(v. 7). That had been God's promise to Adam and Eve in the Garden of Eden, and it was fulfilled with the birth, life, death, and resurrection of Jesus Christ, God's only Son.

PICTURE OF THE SAVIOR

Life Is Nothing Apart from Christ

While it may seem backward and out of place at first glance, David has painted a grisly picture of a life without the light of Christ in order to more gladly sing of the joy found in His embrace. He explains life's total depravity when someone denies God and how this turning away spoils everything he does. Not one of his deeds is good, for the life of a fool displays his lack of faith even if his lips confess God's name. Hopelessness and despair abound for those who seek to substitute something other than Jesus as Lord.

When we confront this inexorable truth through David's psalm, our hearts are drawn back to the hope and fulfillment found in Christ. He redeems us before the Father and calls us into an eternal life full of Him, wherein we find ourselves desiring to share His unfathomable love with the people around us. Thus, the darkness of a Jesus-less existence only serves to display His glorious light all the brighter by contrast.

Who Shall Dwell on Your Holy Hill? (Psalm 15)

What words or phrases stick out to you the most as you read through Psalm 15? Why?

This psalm of David was likely a temple entry prayer that would remind God's people of His holiness. It is reminiscent of the Ten Commandments. None of us is worthy to enter God's presence because of our impure hearts and our sins of word and deed. Yet since we have been forgiven by Christ, we can enter God's presence blameless and holy, asking that God would produce the fruits of His righteousness in our lives.

PICTURE OF THE SAVIOR

Jesus, Our Eternal Temple

From the very beginning of Israel's existence, God had worship standards by which His people were to abide. While observing holy days and honoring Him with song and praise, the Israelites were called to sincere and righteous treatment of one another. Stained by sin, they found themselves far short of God's bar and had to offer sacrifices and perform extra cleansing rites in order to be forgiven and maintain their ability to be with God.

Even today, as we approach the Father in worship, we often find ourselves holding on to sin, and our unrepentance makes us unworthy to be in His presence. Yet the requirements that David listed in this psalm direct our focus to the One sent to fulfill each and every point of God's Law when we never could. Jesus gave Himself up as the atoning sacrifice, dying on the cross and rising again to cover our ugly, dirty sinfulness with His righteousness. In His risen glory, Christ is our temple through which we can always approach God and receive unending grace in faith.

You Will Not Abandon My Soul (Psalm 16)

This psalm begins with a plea for preservation and rescue from God and ends with a glorious expression of hope in life beyond the grave. Many, including the apostles in Acts 2:25 and 13:35, have declared this psalm to be a prophecy of the suffering and resurrection of Jesus Christ.

In the Shadow of Your Wings (Psalm 17)

David pleads for God's protection against a dangerous, bloodthirsty enemy in this psalm. Through no fault of his own, David has suffered the consequences of this broken world. Yet he still hopes that he will behold God's face in righteousness, knowing God will not abandon him.

This psalm powerfully points ahead to Jesus' innocent suffering at the hands of Jewish priests and religious leaders who care nothing for eternal things but only of their power, positions, and prestige in this life. We see Jesus' great hope and confidence that sustained Him on the cross: "As for me, I shall behold Your face in righteousness; when I awake, I shall be satisfied with Your likeness" (Psalm 17:15).

VISUALIZE

The LORD Is My Rock and My Fortress (Psalm 18)

This is a royal thanksgiving hymn in which David expresses both praise and gratitude for God's deliverance from Saul at a time when David knew he could not escape death unless God intervened. He uses powerful, vivid, and epic images to reveal God's victory over His enemies. This was ultimately realized when Jesus Christ came down from heaven and, through His life, death, and resurrection, won victory over sin, death, and the grave for His people.

SET THE SCENE

He Rode on a Cherub

Cherubim (plural of *cherub*) play a prominent role whenever God is revealed in visions in the Scriptures. Two cherubim were carved in the covering of the ark of the covenant, the mercy seat of God; that is, God was enthroned above the cherubim. When Solomon built the temple, he built two enormous cherubim to overshadow the two cherubim on the ark. In Ezekiel 1 and 10, the prophet saw a vision of God coming to call him as prophet and then to abandon the temple because of the idolatry and wickedness taking place there. In both visions, God was seated on His throne, which was being carried and supported by the four cherubim, standing as if in a square. In his Revelation, John saw "four living creatures" (4:6) standing around the throne of God, which are these same cherubim.

When David saw God coming to his rescue, riding on a cherub, we can better understand what he meant.

LINK BETWEEN THE TESTAMENTS

The Lord Is My Fortress → Armor of God (Psalm 18 → Ephesians 6:10–20)

The Scriptures remain constant in how they present the protective and stalwart character of God, even when He has chosen different means to convey this message. For instance, Psalm 18 is a song of praise to God for His mighty protective hand, which rescued David from his enemies. Many great forces of the earth sought to overtake and kill David, but God was greater still and allowed no harm to befall him on account of His love for His children. Couple that with Paul's encouragement in his letter to the Ephesians:

> Finally, be strong in the Lord and in the strength of His might. Put on the whole armor of God, that you may be able to stand against the schemes of the devil. For we do not wrestle against flesh and blood, but against the rulers, against the authorities, against the cosmic powers over this present darkness, against the spiritual forces of evil in the heavenly places. Therefore take up the whole armor of God, that you may be able to withstand in the evil day, and having done all, to stand firm. (Ephesians 6:10–13)

Paul invoked the same trust in God's protection of which David sang to inspire the church in Ephesus in confidence against the fears and troubles that plagued their daily lives.

By using the imagery of armor specially fitted for each believer, Paul personalized God's protection and emphasized Jesus' call to action to "go therefore and make disciples of all nations" (Matthew 28:19) as a heroic quest. The forces that seek to destroy on earth may be powerful and wicked, but our God is Lord over everything and will protect His people of all times and places until His glorious return on the Last Day. Count on it.

What can you learn from David in Psalm 19 about how to devote yourself to meditating on and studying God's Word?

The Law of the LORD Is Perfect (Psalm 19)

In this psalm, David starts by expressing how nature itself declares God's glory and continues by himself praising God for His Word. Though we can begin to see how God's wisdom and might are revealed in nature, we know and understand God's loving, gracious heart only through His revealed Word. We are to continually meditate on and devote ourselves to this Word of God. This Word put on flesh and is our Rock and our Redeemer.

CLEAR THE CONFUSION

What did the psalmist mean in saying, "There is no speech, nor are there words, whose voice is not heard" (v. 3)?

David is teaching us that God has revealed Himself—left evidence of His existence and His handiwork—in His creation, specifically in the daily path of the sun and the way it gives light, heat, and life to all on the earth. Every person on earth can see the sun, no matter what language they might speak. It gives silent witness, without words or speech, but eloquently testifies to the existence of our Creator in a universal language. How sad when people ignore creation's witness and convince themselves it all came into existence through pure chance and evolved over vast spans of time.

Trust in the Name of the LORD Our God (Psalm 20)

This is likely a responsive psalm, in which two groups of people would go back and forth praying the lines together. As such, it may have been offered before King David and his troops went into battle, calling for God's preservation in times of war and conflict.

CLEAR THE CONFUSION

Is it right to pray for victory over other nations in battle?

Many of the psalms include prayers for victory in battle. In the context of ancient Israel, with God's people set aside for a specific purpose in a more or less theocratic government, this would make sense. But what about today? We need to remember a few things. First of all, no one country is the equivalent of ancient Israel, so no country has that same direct role in God's plan. The new Israel is the church, and our ultimate allegiance is to Christ. Also, God does not desire that anyone would die but that all would come to the knowledge of the truth in Christ.

At the same time, we live in a broken world. Until Christ comes, people will hate and wage war against one another. Also, we are to trust that God is able to use earthly authorities to curb wickedness in this world. In times of conflict and war, we are to pray that God would bring about justice and peace and that He would protect those who serve in the armed forces. As God is able to use earthly authorities as His instruments in bringing about this peace, we are to honor our authorities. At the same time, the church should always remember that our final allegiance is to Christ and in the end we are called to serve God rather than man.

The King Rejoices in the LORD's Strength (Psalm 21)

This psalm of David shows the king rejoicing in God's blessings and spurs him on to continually trust in God's strength. Though David himself was anointed by God to be king, this psalm points to the even greater Anointed One, Jesus, who Himself destroyed and swallowed up death, the ultimate enemy of God's people, on the cross.

Why Have You Forsaken Me? (Psalm 22)

This psalm of David expresses the full measure of human emotion when one is confronted with the feeling of being forgotten and abandoned by God, left to be devoured by enemies. Yet in the middle, the tone turns to joy in God's rescue and deliverance. Jesus Christ Himself spoke the opening words of this psalm from the cross (Matthew 27:46), summarizing the entire psalm that had foreshadowed His physical sufferings in incredibly accurate detail. This psalm indicates His pain and joy in enacting God's plan of salvation even as it foreshows His death and His resurrection.

?

How do the overall structure and word choices of Psalm 22 depict the Passion of Jesus Christ?

VISUALIZE

PICTURE OF THE SAVIOR

Christ's Passion

On the cross, Jesus uttered the iconic first line of Psalm 22 (Matthew 27:46), "My God, My God, why have You forsaken Me?" Some commentators think this signals that Jesus recited the whole psalm from the cross, but many do not. Regardless, in reciting this psalm, Jesus points us to understand that what He was doing on the cross was part of God's great plan of salvation. Psalm 22 was not only a song of God's people in their distress but also a prophecy of how Jesus' distress would bring about victory. Jesus, the greater David, experienced the anguish not only of death but also of being forsaken for a time by His Father. Yet like David in the psalm, Jesus, too, was not abandoned forever. The Father rescued Him from the horns of death, and in Christ's victory over the powers of sin and death in the cross and empty tomb, God has revealed His face to all people. As you read through Psalm 22 in its entirety, consider its powerful prophetic role in the plan of salvation. Note the change of tone in the middle of verse 21 that carries through the rest of the psalm. In the final verses, we see a reflection of Jesus' words "It is finished" (John 19:30) and rejoice in His resurrection.

The LORD Is My Shepherd (Psalm 23)

VISUALIZE

WAYPOINT

What is the most memorable phrase or line in Psalm 23 for you? Why is that?

In what ways does Jesus fulfill the role of the shepherd in Psalm 23?

How can this psalm be a comfort to you as you go through the trials of life? Where can you place a copy of this psalm for your own ongoing study?

What does this text show us?

Each line of this short psalm is iconic, etched into the fabric of our Christian lives through repetition at funerals and other times of mourning. It compares the life of God's people to that of sheep under the watch and protection of a good shepherd. Since David was a shepherd before he became king, he understood the importance and value of a loving and faithful shepherd. God's care for David and all His people is exponentially greater.

What does this text reveal about God's plan of salvation?

The theme of sheep and shepherds is constant throughout the Scriptures. Abel, the second human born on earth, tended sheep (Genesis 4:2), as did Abraham, Isaac, Jacob, Moses, David, and so many others. Naturally, the relationship between sheep and shepherd became one of the most common, if not the central, metaphors in the Old Testament for the relationship between God and His people. Psalm 23 highlights this relationship so well. Whereas we, like sheep, are vulnerable and prone to wander, God lovingly leads us through the darkness of this world to our eternal home. Jesus referred to Himself as the Good Shepherd (John 10). Through His death and resurrection, He—the Son of David—fulfills the role of the Good Shepherd in Psalm 23, giving us a place in His heavenly home forever.

What does this text uncover about our identity and calling as God's people today?

This world is a scary and often troubling place. There is so much to fear. Yet Jesus promises to be with us, even to the end of the age. By the power of the Spirit living in us, Jesus dwells with us. We are His, now and forever. This is our identity, and we can find great comfort in all circumstances by returning to God's Word and meditating upon it.

LINK BETWEEN THE TESTAMENTS

The Lord Is My Shepherd → I Am the Good Shepherd (Psalm 23 → John 10:11–18)

Often the shortest psalms are jam-packed with biblical truth, and Psalm 23 is certainly no exception. David gave thanks for God's loving care, which provided all that he needed for a bountiful life of worship and reverence for God. He described this relationship as that of a shepherd and his sheep, paying homage to the utter dependence the sheep has on the shepherd and applying the idea of the sheep to himself.

In the New Testament, Jesus identified Himself as God's Son, who had personally come to shepherd His sheep. When young David asked King Saul's permission to be his representative to fight Israel, David mentioned how he had laid down his life to rescue his sheep from lions and bears and that God had rescued him. Jesus expressed His willingness to lay down His life for His sheep, not only to die for us but also to rise again and be our living Good Shepherd forever.

The King of Glory (Psalm 24)

This psalm of David may have been written when David brought the ark of the covenant up into Jerusalem (2 Samuel 6:12–15). This psalm offers a wonderful way to prepare as we approach worship. It starts by asserting the majesty and glory of God, something we as sinners can easily forget as we approach His presence for worship. It asks and answers who may come into God's presence: only those whose hearts and hands are pure because God Himself has removed their sins. Then it turns to focus on God, who comes to us in Word and Sacrament, the Lord who saved us by His life, death, and resurrection.

CLEAR THE CONFUSION

What Gates and Ancient Doors Was David Referring To?

What are the gates and doors that are to lift up their heads? Was David talking about the gates and doors of the tabernacle? Would they be the doors of the temple when his son Solomon built them in Jerusalem? Are they the doors of our churches and places of worship? Or are they the gates of heaven itself?

The answer is yes to all. The God who created the heavens and the earth is unapproachable to sinful humans trapped in our sin. Our way is barred by the doors of God's holy presence. But God humbled Himself to come down to us in the incarnation and birth of His Son, Jesus Christ. Jesus has given us His righteousness through faith, and we have access to go up to God in our local places of worship—and at the end of our earthly lives, to go up to God's throne room in heaven.

But even more than that, God comes down to us through His Word and Sacraments in our church homes. May we remember anew the grace of our God and the tremendous honor of standing in the Lord's house to receive His gracious gifts.

Teach Me Your Paths (Psalm 25)

In this psalm, David prays not only for deliverance from his enemies but also for forgiveness of sins and instruction in God's ways. Oppressed by the ancient enemies of sin, death, and the devil, we, too, pray for God's deliverance and rejoice in the forgiveness of sins and our guidance in God's truth through His Word.

Verse 1 has been incorporated into the opening sentences of our Communion liturgy (*LSB*, p. 160):

P: Lift up your hearts.

C: We lift them to the Lord.

I Will Bless the LORD (Psalm 26)

Here, David contrasts the emotions of being falsely accused of wrongdoing with the joy of worship. Amid the accusations and influences of the devil, God's people find their refuge in God's truth and in God's faithfulness to us. This may have been meant to be sung by worshipers as they entered the temple gates.

CLEAR THE CONFUSION

What is vindication?

Vindication is being proven innocent when falsely accused. The clearest case in the Scriptures is Jesus' resurrection. When He was condemned and nailed to the cross, the Jewish leaders and Jewish people mocked and ridiculed Him, convinced that He must have been a fake and a fraud or else God surely would not have subjected the true Messiah to such horrific and shameful suffering.

Jesus did not defend Himself or His honor either during His trials or on the cross. He trusted His Father to vindicate Him, which God did by raising Him from the dead on the third day. That vindication will be complete when Christ returns on the Last Day to judge the world, and all those who pierced Him will look upon Him seated on His judgment seat in great power and glory.

When we are falsely accused, we do not need to worry about defending ourselves. It is best to let God vindicate us in the way and the time that He chooses.

The LORD Is My Light and My Salvation (Psalm 27)

In the first half of this psalm, David confidently rejoices in God's protection. In the second half, David cries out to God for help, forgiveness, and guidance. This may have been a psalm used during the worship liturgy of ancient Israel, with sacrifices being offered at the midpoint. The Lord's tent, which David mentions in verses 5 and 6, is the tabernacle.

The LORD Is My Strength and My Shield (Psalm 28)

We read another psalm of David written during a time of personal crisis, perhaps the time when Absalom rebelled against him (2 Samuel 15–18). The psalmist is troubled, and realizing he cannot save himself, he calls upon God to be his strength and shield, not only for him but also for all of God's people.

Ascribe to the LORD Glory (Psalm 29)

This psalm focuses on the voice of God, which God used to create the heavens and the earth and through which He also creates faith and saves us from our sins. In this psalm, creation responds to the voice of its Creator, and the sound of God's voice unleashes a great flood that destroys the earth (Genesis 6–9). God's power over creation is absolute, and all glory belongs to Him. Later interpreters have read this as a prophecy of the Gospel, with the waters of the flood representing the waters of Baptism, through which God drowns the old self and raises the new self to life.

?

In what ways do the words and phrases of Psalm 29 point us back to the nature and blessing of Baptism?

Joy Comes with the Morning (Psalm 30)

After a period of great sorrow caused by his sin, David expresses his joy in God's forgiveness and restoration. This came after David's sinful census and the wrath that ensued (2 Samuel 24). At the very spot where the angel of the Lord had shown him mercy and stopped the plague on Israel, David built an altar and planned for the temple to be built.

First Chronicles 22–29 shows us that David made many preparations to assist his son Solomon in building the temple, from the design itself, to stockpiles of materials, to organizing the priests and Levites who served as guards and musicians for the temple. He likely wrote this psalm to dedicate that land on which Solomon would build the temple.

LINK BETWEEN THE TESTAMENTS

Joy Comes in the Morning → Christ, Our Hope (Psalm 30 → James 1:2–4)

In response to the great mercy God showed to him, David may have written this psalm as a dedication of the worship site that would eventually become Jerusalem's mighty temple (see 2 Samuel 24:25; 1 Chronicles 21:26). David learned that even the greatest sorrow, whether brought about by outside forces or one's own hand, would yield to the joy of God's deliverance in due time.

James would later pen his letter to the early churches with the same topic for his introduction: "Count it all joy, my brothers, when you meet trials of various kinds, for you know that the testing of your faith produces steadfastness. And let steadfastness have its full effect, that you may be perfect and complete, lacking in nothing" (James 1:2–4). The troubles of the moment are just as much in God's hands as the triumphs of the next; God works both for our good and for His glory. With this understanding given throughout the Scriptures, we can persevere in whatever trials the enemy seeks to put in our way and have the utmost joy in the promise fulfilled for our salvation through Christ alone.

What does Psalm 31 further uncover for us about how we are to understand Jesus' death on the cross?

Into Your Hand I Commit My Spirit (Psalm 31)

This psalm of David was possibly written in response to his being pursued by Saul (1 Samuel 23). In it, David denounces those who worship idols and extols the virtues of trusting in the one true God. God is faithful and good, and He delivers us from our ancient enemies. Jesus spoke the words of verse 5 from the cross, His final words before dying for the sins of the world (Luke 23:46).

Blessed Are the Forgiven (Psalm 32)

This classic penitential psalm shows the value of honestly examining our lives according to God's Law, repenting of our sins, and then rejoicing in the blessing that is forgiveness. This psalm of repentance has been used throughout the millennia as part of the corporate worship life of God's people in Confession and Absolution.

CLEAR THE CONFUSION

How should we understand Confession and Absolution?

There are several psalms that focus on the role of repentance. Among the most memorable are Psalm 32 and Psalm 51. In the Divine Service, Christians practice something called *corporate Confession and Absolution*. When we speak together the words of confession of sins, it often sounds like the words (or directly includes the words) of a psalm. God wants us to confess our sins to Him. Even more, He wants us to hear that our sins are forgiven in Christ. After His resurrection, Jesus appeared to His disciples, "breathed on them and said to them, 'Receive the Holy Spirit. If you forgive the sins of any, they are forgiven them; if you withhold forgiveness from any, it is withheld'" (John 20:22–23). In this amazing promise, Jesus gave the church the power to speak words of forgiveness as if they were the very words of Christ. As Christians, we have a great privilege to be able to confess our sins to God and to hear the words of forgiveness. This repentance is a central aspect of the Christian life, and it is a great gift to receive the absolution.

The Steadfast Love of the LORD (Psalm 33)

This psalm breaks the pattern we have seen thus far in the book, as it is not a psalm that was explicitly, or implicitly, attributed to David. Instead, the reference to "a new song" (v. 3) likely points to a later date of composition, perhaps at the time of Jehoshaphat or Hezekiah, hundreds of years after David.

The psalmist focuses our attention on the power of God's words. By His spoken Word, He created and ordered all things. His counsel stands true and good for all generations. This psalm praises God for something new and wonderful He has done, perhaps a national deliverance from enemies. It admonishes the hearers to put their trust in God, not in armies and war horses, for help and salvation.

Compare Psalm 33 to previous psalms of David. In what ways are they similar in their content and their tone? How are they different?

CLEAR THE CONFUSION

Who wrote the book of Psalms?

As the official songbook of God's people was composed over a thousand years (as was mentioned briefly in the introduction to the Psalms above), it is understandable that the psalms were compiled from many sources and authors. The most prominent and prolific author was David, who is attributed to seventy-three of the psalms, though he may have written more. Other authors include Asaph, a Levite whom David appointed as one of the court musicians (1 Chronicles 6:31–32, 39; 25:1–2), who may have written twelve or so. The sons of Korah, a group of Levites, have eleven psalms attributed to them. Solomon, the son of David, is associated with two psalms; and Moses, Heman, Ethan, and Jeduthun have one ascribed to each of them. In addition to these, many of the psalms are anonymous. They represent a wealth of experience and variety in authorship across time, which adds to the rich texture of this impressive book of the Bible.

We see more of this rich texture and wealth of experience and variety in our hymnals, as authors from the centuries have composed deep poetry to call upon God in trouble, to praise Him for His faithfulness, and to remember and celebrate the great deeds of salvation accomplished by our Lord and Savior, Jesus Christ.

Taste and See That the LORD Is Good (Psalm 34)

The text of this psalm refers to an event when David fled from Saul's army into the city of Gath of the Philistines, recorded in 1 Samuel 21:10–15. When the king of Gath learned that this was the same David who had led Israel's army in battle against the Philistines for Saul, David pretended to be insane to escape capture. In this psalm, David lauds the Lord and praises Him for delivering and redeeming the life of His servants.

Great Is the LORD (Psalm 35)

This psalm of David was likely written during a time when he was running from Saul and some of his own followers turned against him. David calls on God as a righteous judge, asking the Lord to bring his accusers to shame and dishonor. This is the first of what is known as the *imprecatory psalms*, in which the author calls down a curse and prays for the defeat of an enemy.

CLEAR THE CONFUSION

What about the "bad" psalms?

There are a series of psalms known as the *imprecatory*, or cursing, psalms, which are honestly troubling for many modern readers. This is understandable, as Jesus has commanded us to love and serve our neighbor, even our enemies, not to ask God to curse them.

The book of Psalms does cover the entire range of human emotion, and frustration and righteous anger are part of that. The best way for modern readers to interpret these psalms, and to use them in our prayers, is to focus on the eternal enemies of God's people: the devil, the world, and our sinful flesh as the enemies we are praying against. Like the psalmists, we can pray not only that God would deliver us from evil but also that God would destroy those wicked things that oppose Him and His kingdom. Christ will return and accomplish this at the final judgment.

How Precious Is Your Steadfast Love (Psalm 36)

The superscription of this psalm of David shows how David was a leader and instructor of the people. In this psalm, he contrasts the wicked with God's protection of His children by faith. He shows how the failure to fear God (that is, take His wrath and judgment seriously) leads the wicked to plot evil and trouble because they think they will never be discovered. But lest we become terrified by the plotting of evildoers, David reminds us that God's love for us is steadfast, unmovable. He will protect His children from being destroyed by the plots of the wicked and will bring us into His eternal presence.

CLEAR THE CONFUSION

What is meant by the phrase "he plots trouble while on his bed" (v. 4)?

The wicked are unable to rest at night because they are plotting how to do evil and get away with it. They lie there plotting the "perfect crime," never realizing that God knows their thoughts and is witness to all their deeds. Even if they never face earthly judgment and punishment, God will surely expose their wicked intention and punish their sins on Judgment Day unless they repent and put their trust in Christ their Savior.

He Will Not Forsake His Saints (Psalm 37)

You will notice none of the verses of this psalm focus on God or what God does; instead they focus on what believers do with God's help. David lays out the road of life and encourages us to continue in the way of faith and not to depart from it. If we do that by God's power and help until the very end of our lives, we will enjoy eternal life for Jesus' sake.

In this psalm, David counsels us not to judge by outward appearance or to fret when we see evildoers prosper in this world while believers struggle. David encourages us to look at the big picture, to look from God's perspective. Evildoers prosper only for a brief time, then God calls them to account. When we find ourselves fretting that there is no advantage in believing and in depriving ourselves of this world's sinful pleasures, this psalm reminds us that in God's appointed time, His divine punishment will fall on the wicked, but God will never forsake those whom He has made righteous by faith.

Do Not Forsake Me, O LORD (Psalm 38)

In this penitential psalm, or psalm of repentance, David compares the agony of his sins to a plague, in which he suffers extreme physical suffering. He offers up the psalm as part of the memorial offering (Leviticus 24:7) as he repents of his sins. David makes a distinction between sins of which we have not repented to God and those of which we have repented. It is the unrepented sins that weigh us down and crush us, causing psychological and even physical harm. Through our

How do words and phrases from Psalm 38 serve as a model for us in our repentance?

confession, Jesus takes those sins away from us and carries them on His own shoulders to the cross.

CLEAR THE CONFUSION

What did David mean when he said, "I am like a deaf man" and "like a mute man" (v. 13)?

David was speaking of false friends who were now betraying him. They were slandering him and telling lies about him. He had no answer for their false charges and relied on God, who knows the truth and would vindicate him. This can remind us of Jesus, who stood silent during His trials while the Jewish priests and leaders stood by vehemently accusing Him. Instead of defending Himself, Jesus stood as if He were deaf to their charges and mute, unable to answer them. Instead, Jesus waited patiently for His Father to vindicate Him.

What Is the Measure of My Days? (Psalm 39)

This psalm of David is written for Jeduthun, one of David's three court musicians (2 Chronicles 5:12). In it, the psalmist is facing a horrible spiritual dilemma that strikes many people, such as Job: Where is God in the midst of my suffering? Why won't He answer me and give me relief?

The psalmist is a devout believer, earnestly trying to live a life pleasing to God. He even restrains his tongue to keep from sinning, especially in the presence of the wicked. But the seeming injustice of his situation finally burns deep inside until he must speak, whether it be a sin or not. When he does speak, it sounds like Solomon's book of Ecclesiastes. Our lives are so, so short, and we go about like a shadow, working and heaping things up and never knowing who will have them when we die and are gone. It is all vanity.

In verse 12, he asks God to listen to his cry and to forgive and restore him. In verse 13, he asks God to look away and leave him alone that he may know a moment of happiness before it is all over and he dies. He ends the psalm still in confusion.

This is such a powerful and useful psalm for times in our lives when we are suffering, there is no end in sight, and God seems far away—as during long-standing relationship struggles, in the midst of financial difficulties that seem to keep getting worse and worse, or while struggling through chemotherapy treatments. Life in this fallen world is sometimes painful and confusing, and there are moments when all we can do is pour out our hearts to God, expressing our pain, confusion, and heartbreak. In those times when we don't know what to pray, "the [Holy] Spirit Himself intercedes for us with groanings too deep for words" (Romans 8:26).

My Help and My Deliverer (Psalm 40)

Psalm 39 spoke to those times in life when we are in the middle of a crisis and see no resolution. This psalm is perfect for the time after God has answered our prayer and has brought us a time of relief and peace.

It may have originated in David's earlier years when he was being pursued by Saul. He cried out for rescue and deliverance, not trusting in his own goodness or works, and God delivered him so he could enjoy a time of peace and security. But once again, trouble has come upon him. Likewise, today we find our security and peace in the great deliverer, Jesus Christ.

PICTURE OF THE SAVIOR

"Behold, I have come; . . . I delight to do Your will, O my God." (Psalm 40:7–8)

This passage from Psalm 40 is quoted in Hebrews 10:1–10 (v. 7) to show that all the Old Testament sacrifices pointed ahead to Jesus' willing offering of His life on the cross for our sins. Apart from Jesus, those sacrifices were vain and powerless to help the Israelites in the Old Testament. At the same time, without true repentance and faith in God's promised Savior, the offering of those sacrifices and performance of works were also vain and could not forgive sins.

O LORD, Be Gracious to Me (Psalm 41)

Likely composed by David during the time of Absalom's rebellion (2 Samuel 15–18), this psalm reveals the great sickness and agony that David experienced at the treason of those who once called him king. Pouring out his soul, the psalmist calls out for God's gracious restoration.

?

Many of David's psalms mention the anguish of betrayal by friends. According to Psalm 41 and your own experience, what makes treason and betrayal so painful for us? What can we learn from David about properly turning to God in our anguish?

PICTURE OF THE SAVIOR

"I am not speaking of all of you; I know whom I have chosen. But the Scripture will be fulfilled, 'He who ate My bread has lifted his heel against Me.'" (John 13:18; Jesus quoting Psalm 41:9)

When David's son Absalom rose against him and tried to steal the throne, one of the greatest blows to David was learning his trusted adviser Ahithophel, who had shared meals at David's table, was one of the architects of that rebellion and was the biggest reason for its initial success.

Jesus suffered a similar betrayal when one of His twelve chosen disciples, Judas, who sat at Jesus' table and ate bread from Jesus' hands, rose up against Him and betrayed Him to the Jewish religious authorities with a kiss. This makes Psalm 41 messianic because in it David foreshadows Jesus' ministry, betrayal, crucifixion, and resurrection.

LINK BETWEEN THE TESTAMENTS

God, Be Gracious to Me → Jesus Heals (Psalm 41 → Luke 5:17–26)

Have you ever been ill at the most inconvenient time and felt frustrated because it precluded you from doing what you needed to do? David echoes that sentiment vividly in Psalm 41 and reminds us of the deeper rot in our hearts. The great king of Israel had fallen sick and felt especially pressured and hemmed-in by his enemies as he was writing it. David recognized that beneath his frantic concerns over the visible conditions in his life, he was suffering from a much graver condition: a sinful nature. He devoted much of his psalm to this topic, asking for forgiveness and restoration so that he might serve God dutifully. Healing was and continued to be a necessity.

In the Gospel of Luke, Jesus encountered a paralyzed man whose friends brought him to Jesus:

> And behold, some men were bringing on a bed a man who was paralyzed, and they were seeking to bring him in and lay him before Jesus, but finding no way to bring him in, because of the crowd, they went up on the roof and let him down with his bed through the tiles into the midst before Jesus. And when He saw their faith, He said, "Man, your sins are forgiven you. . . . I say to you, rise, pick up your bed and go home." And immediately he rose up before them and picked up what he had been lying on and went home, glorifying God. (Luke 5:18–20, 24–25)

The man who was paralyzed recognized that Jesus was exactly who he needed and no other. Jesus first attended to the sickness of his heart by forgiving his sins, then granted him the physical healing he sought, and later so much more by His death and resurrection on the cross—the same healing David had received so long ago.

Book Two, Mostly Psalms of David About the Kingdom (Psalms 42–72)

Both the first and second books (divisions) of the Psalms are dominated by writings of David. Whereas Book One included mostly personal songs of David, Book Two revolves mostly around nationalistic psalms during the reign of the kings.

Why Are You Cast Down, O My Soul? (Psalm 42)

Psalms 42 and 43 are presented in a way that indicates they are meant to be understood together. Psalm 42 is the first psalm in the book not specifically attributed to David but to the sons of Korah. In this psalm, the writer expresses a deep desire to come to God's temple, comparing his longing to that of a deer panting for flowing streams. Though it would seem like the wicked and godless win, and though our souls are in turmoil within us, we hope in God's victory won for us in Christ.

?

What events in life have caused you to experience this intense spiritual thirst to come to God's house, to seek His face, to hear His Word, to receive His Sacraments, and to know He is here for you?

VISUALIZE

SETTING THE SCENE

The Sons of Korah

The sons of Korah were, collectively, descendents of Korah the Levite (Numbers 16). Though Korah rebelled against Moses and Aaron and suffered a horrendous death, God was merciful to his believing descendants, whom He placed in charge of the threshold of the tent of meeting (1 Chronicles 9:19). They would also serve in this function after the construction of the temple. This group is responsible for eleven psalms, written around the times of David and Solomon.

What can you learn about praying for God's guidance from the short yet powerful Psalm 43?

Send Out Your Light and Your Truth (Psalm 43)

Continuing from Psalm 42, the psalmist again asks his soul why it is cast down. The obvious answer is that he is being treated unjustly. Even so, the psalmist cries out for God's light and truth to lead him. God's Word is that light for God's people, illuminating Christ and leading us in the truth.

Come to Our Help (Psalm 44)

This psalm vividly expresses the emotional anguish of God's people when they experience defeat or oppression. The psalmist speaks of the people's faithfulness to God and wonders why God allows the enemies of His people to prevail over them. Just as God's people today experience opposition and tribulation, so we, too, are tempted to despair of God's presence. Yet in Christ we can be assured that God will never abandon us.

LINK BETWEEN THE TESTAMENTS

"For Your sake we are killed all the day long; we are regarded as sheep to be slaughtered." (Psalm 44:22 → Romans 8:36)

Throughout the Old Testament, there were certainly times when Israel deserved to suffer at the hands of enemy nations because they rebelled against God and worshiped foreign gods. But in this psalm, Israel had been faithful to God and yet still suffered invasion and defeat. Such events happened in the days of Hezekiah, the righteous king of Judah (see 2 Kings 18–19).

Paul refers to these words in the eighth chapter of his letter to the Christians in Rome. In this powerful chapter, Paul is teaching us to find comfort in all our sufferings by remembering that the Holy Spirit, who dwells in us, intercedes for us; God the Father makes all things work together for our good; and Jesus is at the right hand of the Father, interceding for us.

Your Throne, O God, Is Forever (Psalm 45)

This psalm of the sons of Korah depicts a wedding celebration of a great king to his bride. Though this may have been written for a specific, unnamed king during the history of the kings of Israel, in a greater way, it is a prophecy of the Gospel and the kingdom of Christ. Christ is the Anointed One, the King of kings, and the church is His Bride.

PICTURE OF THE SAVIOR

The Royal Wedding

The unification and joyous harmony found in a royal wedding illustrate a fraction of the joy in the reunion of Christ and His Bride, the church, and create a helpful image of Him and the hope we have in His return. The sons of Korah describe the splendor of the groom in great detail, noting His simultaneous humanity and exalted might and power revealed in His actions: speaking grace and fighting valiantly for the lives of His people. Anointed by God with the Spirit in full, this Bridegroom is Christ, the Son of God, who became flesh to rescue His Bride, the church, dressed in the riches and beauty of His righteousness. We are welcomed with open arms into His kingdom because of His mighty victory over sin, death, and the power of the devil on the cross. Therefore, we can revel in the joy of our salvation and celebrate in eager expectation of His great wedding as we recognize the earthly marriages of our friends and family.

God Is Our Fortress (Psalm 46)

WAYPOINT

What does this text show us?
This psalm of the sons of Korah may have been written to be sung without an accompaniment. It is about trusting God in the face of great crises, including natural disasters and wars. Even though these things assail God's people, God is in the midst of them in His temple. The fallen powers of the devil, the world, and our sinful flesh have no option but to "be still" before God (v. 10), who is our strength, help, and fortress.

If you had to depict this psalm in a series of images, what pictures would you use? How would you arrange them?

What difference does it make in your daily life that Jesus became human, lived among us, and lives among us still?

How does this psalm offer you comfort in your specific daily needs and struggles?

What does this text reveal about God's plan of salvation?
Throughout God's epic plan of salvation, we see God choosing to dwell with His people. Though omnipotent, omniscient, and omnipresent, God is not distant. He comes near to His people. He came near to Abraham as the Angel of the Lord, wrestled with Jacob, guided Israel in the wilderness by the pillars of cloud and fire, and dwelled above the mercy seat over the ark of the covenant in the temple during the time this psalm was written. Even so, God is holy and humanity is sinful, and God's presence in these and other instances was always accompanied by fear.

Yet in the fullness of time, the Son of God took on human flesh permanently and made His dwelling among His people. Jesus came in humility, born of a woman, born under the Law, to redeem those who were under the Law, to make us His sons and daughters. Through the cross and the empty tomb, the One who came to dwell with us conquered sin, death, and hell for us. At Pentecost, He sent the Holy Spirit to dwell among us, confirming His promise to be with us always, to the end of the age. Christ is our fortress, now and forever.

What does this text uncover about our identity and calling as God's people today?
During troubling times, especially times of scarcity, natural disaster, or opposition, it's easy to feel like God is far away. This psalm not only points us to God's presence in our midst but also reminds us that Christ is our fortress and strength. Through the Spirit, Christ is with us always and continues to strengthen our faith through Word and Sacrament. All creation has no authority ahead of Christ. We can rejoice that He is our mighty fortress, now and forever, and will never leave us or forsake us, however we may feel.

LINK BETWEEN THE TESTAMENTS

God Is Our Fortress → God's Everlasting Love (Psalm 46 → Romans 8:31–39)

As the inspiration for Martin Luther's most famous hymn, "A Mighty Fortress Is Our God," Psalm 46 boldly declares how our God stands firm against the chaos and competing forces present in the world. No matter what may threaten our wealth, relationships, and lives, God will be a bulwark under which we can find refuge, the psalmists proudly sing.

Paul holds firmly to this belief too, as revealed in his words to the Romans: "For I am sure that neither death nor life, nor angels nor rulers, nor things present nor things to come, nor powers, nor height nor depth, nor anything else in all creation, will be able to separate us from the love of God in Christ Jesus our Lord" (Romans 8:38–39). The promise that God alone, the King of the universe, will protect and preserve His people has given hope to His church for thousands of years, to Jews and Gentiles alike, and has been fulfilled in the coming of Jesus, who took mankind's sin upon Himself so that we would be spared the sting of death and be reunited with Him forevermore.

God Is King over All the Earth (Psalm 47)

This psalm of the sons of Korah praises God for all He has done for His people. The psalm reminds us that God is the great King over His people—Israel in the Old Testament and the Christian Church in these New Testament times. But He also reigns over His entire creation, every nation, tongue, and people group. Today we can echo the words of this psalm as a great Gospel shout, proclaiming God's faithfulness to fulfill His promises to His people from Abraham to Jacob to Christ to us today.

Zion, the City of Our God (Psalm 48)

This psalm continues the theme of using a fortress as a symbol of God's strength and protection for His people. God is in the midst of His people, and He will remain their strength and shield forever. Because of God's firm and eternal mercy, we can confidently tell the next generations of our God.

Why Should I Fear in Times of Trouble? (Psalm 49)

In Psalm 49, the sons of Korah point out a stark and unavoidable fact of life in this fallen world: wealth and earthly success cannot overcome death (the place of death is commonly called Sheol). Regardless of socioeconomic status or wisdom, all lives end in death. God alone has the power to ransom our souls from death, and He has done so through Christ.

PICTURE OF THE SAVIOR

"Truly no man can ransom another." (Psalm 49:7)

This psalm speaks of the futility and vanity of wealth, in which so many people place their trust. Whether a millionaire or a billionaire, no matter how such a person is able to amass fortune, it will mean absolutely nothing when this earthly life ends and that individual must stand before the judgment seat of Christ and give account for his or her life.

Only One can ransom another, and that is the spotless Lamb of God, Jesus Christ. The Son of God became human to take our guilt and sin upon Himself and to offer His life on the cross as the ransom for our sins. Only in Jesus Christ are we rescued from death and hell. God be praised for providing that ransom in His one and only Son.

God Himself Is Judge (Psalm 50)

Here we see the first psalm written by Asaph, one of the Levites appointed by David to create music for the temple services (1 Chronicles 15:16–24). In this psalm, we see God reprimand His people for relying on empty rituals and sacrifices in worship while ignoring sins. Though God delights in our faithful offerings, which are responses of thanksgiving for His full and free forgiveness, they are no replacement for true repentance, which leads to confession and absolution.

Create in Me a Clean Heart, O God (Psalm 51)

VISUALIZE

"Purge me with hyssop,
and I shall be clean;
wash me, and I shall be whiter than
snow." (Psalm 51:7)

The Israelites used hyssop plants to paint their doorways with blood so the angel of death would pass over their homes. Hyssop was also used in ceremonial cleansings to indicate God's forgiveness of sins.

WAYPOINT

What does this text show us?

More than most psalms, this one was written in reference to a specific event. After King David had not only committed adultery with Bathsheba but also ordered her husband's murder and covered it up as a casualty of war, God confronted David of his sin through the prophet Nathan. David wrote this psalm in response, pouring out his confession of sins and guilt before God. He calls for God's mercy and forgiveness, asking for a new heart and boldly promising to change his ways. In all of this, David appeals to God's mercy and faithfulness to His promises rather than to his own goodness or past obedience.

?

What specific words or phrases from this psalm help you understand the nature of sin and true repentance?

What does this text reveal about God's plan of salvation?
This psalm sits at a critical point in the life of David. He had been chosen by God to be king over Israel. The Bible calls him a man after God's heart (1 Samuel 13:14; Acts 13:22). David wrote many of the psalms in this very book, and one of the most common names for the awaited Messiah would be Son of David. Yet here, after such great sin, David had been caught red-handed by God. Without Jesus' bloody atonement on the cross and God the Father's forgiveness and mercy, the king would be worthy only of the fires of hell. Yet even to these grievous sins by the anointed head of God's people, God brought about repentance and forgiveness of sins. God is able to call all people back to repentance and faith through His mighty Word.

What does this text uncover about our identity and calling as God's people today?
Portions of this psalm have served as an important text in corporate worship for hundreds of years. Even if we do not have the same kind of experiences as David, we, too, bear the burden of sin. Without God's forgiveness and mercy, we would have no hope of eternal life. But with Christ, there is forgiveness and life. We can daily die to sin and rise to new life in Him, who creates in us clean and pure hearts. So as we go through life, we not only confess our sins and receive forgiveness, but we also rejoice and praise God for His mercy.

?

What does this psalm reveal to you about the nature of God's grace?

?

How can you use this psalm as a model for your own prayer life?

CLEAR THE CONFUSION

Why did David say, "Against You, You only, have I sinned" (v. 4), when he also sinned against Uriah and Bathsheba?

Every sin we commit against another person is ultimately and chiefly a sin against God, who created that person and brought him or her into our life to love and serve. David's sin against Uriah was great, but his sin against God was far greater because he showed his ingratitude to God by not being content with the wives God had provided for him. David could never undo the crime he committed against Uriah or pay Bathsheba back for what he had taken from her. Even more, he could not pay God back for his sin. But God would provide His own Son, Jesus, David's descendant, to take David's guilt and punishment away forever by taking it upon Himself when He suffered and died on the cross.

The Steadfast Love of God Endures (Psalm 52)

Like Psalm 51, this psalm was written in response to a specific occasion. When David first fled from King Saul, he had received help from the priest Ahimelech. After a man from Edom named Doeg told of this to Saul, Saul ordered Doeg to kill Ahimelech, his family, eighty-five priests, and the whole city of Nob (1 Samuel 22:6–23). Psalm 52 is David's deep lament over the needless and evil slaughter of so many. It especially focuses on Doeg's evil tongue, which preyed upon Saul's suspicions and for personal favors was willing to wipe out a city of priests. Though evil may appear unstoppable, we know that in the end evil is overcome and cannot win. Christ overcame the evil powers for us on the cross.

There Is None Who Does Good (Psalm 53)

Once again, David returns in Psalm 53 to the recurring theme in the psalms of wisdom and foolishness. Here he addresses the "fool" who says that there is no God. In this broken world, there are so many who boldly claim that there is no God. These atheists will be rejected if they do not repent. Yet in the midst of these fools, God's people are to place our hope in the God of Israel, trusting in His salvation.

LINK BETWEEN THE TESTAMENTS

"There is none who does good, not even one" →
"None is righteous" (Psalm 53:3 → Romans 3:10)

The psalmist points out that because of our sinful nature, all of us act as if there were no God when we sin in thought, word, and deed. Paul repeated that same point in the first three chapters of the book of Romans. In the first chapter, he exposed the sinfulness of the Gentiles. In the second chapter, he exposed the sins of the Jews. Early in the third chapter, he showed that every single person is a sinner and no one is righteous, not even a single person. But then he went on to show that God had sent His Son out of Zion. Jesus Christ is the Righteous One, who took our sin and guilt upon Himself and won our salvation on the cross.

The Lord Upholds My Life (Psalm 54)

Returning to psalms written for specific occasions, Psalm 54 recounts the time when David hid from the murderous Saul in the wilderness of Ziph in southern Judah. The people of Ziph betrayed David, hoping to win favor with Saul by revealing David's location (1 Samuel 23:15–24; 26:1). David calls not only for God's help but also for God's justice against those who betray God's anointed. In the end, we know there will be justice for sin, and only those who are called to be God's people through Christ will receive salvation.

CLEAR THE CONFUSION

Why do many of the psalms refer to specific events in time rather than general and abstract events?

Often, when we think of hymns or songs, our first thought is to consider how they apply to our own lives. Though this is not bad, it is easy to forget that these were written by real people in real earthly circumstances in history. The context of the events in their lives influenced the writing. The same goes for the psalms. These were written by real people in history, who dealt with real human emotions and problems. The events listed in the superscriptions of certain psalms only add to our understanding of the rich tapestry of God's Word. Even so, we are to understand that the psalms are timeless and inspired by the Holy Spirit, so they are all useful for our prayer and meditation.

Cast Your Burden on the LORD (Psalm 55)

From inferences in the text, this psalm was written at a time when David had experienced a betrayal from someone close to him. No specific event is named, but David certainly felt this kind of deep betrayal when his trusted adviser Ahithophel conspired with his son Absalom, who sought to usurp his throne and end his life. Whether David wrote the psalm because of that occasion or not, the words of the psalm also describe the pain Jesus felt from Judas's betrayal. In the midst of his horrid experience, David calls upon the Lord in prayer, casting his cares and anxieties on God. We, too, can follow David's example in attitude and in prayer.

?

Using David's example in Psalm 55, what are some burdens that you can cast before the Lord in prayer today?

VISUALIZE

In God I Trust (Psalm 56)

Like Psalm 34, this song appears to have been composed during a time when David pretended to be insane while he was hiding from Saul in the Philistine city of Gath (1 Samuel 21:10–15). Threatened by danger on all sides, in the very presence of his enemies, David expresses great thanks and praise to God for His protection and all that He has provided.

Let Your Glory Be over All the Earth (Psalm 57)

The occasion for this psalm follows closely after the occasion for Psalm 56. After hiding from Saul in Gath, David then hides from Saul in the cave of Adullam (1 Samuel 22:1–2). There he writes this psalm, in which he once again cries out to God for help while praising God for His faithfulness.

God Who Judges the Earth (Psalm 58)

Though not noted in the text, Psalm 58's similarities to Psalm 57 make it a likely companion psalm, perhaps written on the same occasion. Here, David calls for God's righteous vengeance and punishment against the wicked.

David wants other people to see God's justice and give God glory for judging rightly, protecting the innocent, and punishing the guilty.

Deliver Me from My Enemies (Psalm 59)

The superscription of this psalm says David composed it "when Saul sent men to watch his house in order to kill him." This fits well the event recorded in 1 Samuel 19:11–12, when Saul's daughter Michal, who had married David, let him down by a rope through the window and rescued him. In the first half of the psalm, David offers up a prayer, and in the second half, he reflects on God's deliverance. As we navigate life, pursued by the ancient enemies of the devil, the world, and our flesh, we, too, can both pray for rescue in current circumstances and rejoice in God's eternal victory.

What words or phrases stick out to you from Psalm 59? Why?

LINK BETWEEN THE TESTAMENTS

Deliver Me from My Enemies → God's Kingdom (Psalm 59 → John 18:33–37)

Psalm 59 underscores the impermanence of man's kingdoms when compared to God's eternal reign over mankind. David's cry for help against those who sought to defame and even kill him transforms into a declaration of God's supremacy over His enemies as the poem progresses. As this shift occurs, David delights in the fact that "God rules over Jacob to the ends of the earth" (v. 13) and "hold[s] all the nations in derision" (v. 8).

Jesus revealed the other half of this good news to Pontius Pilate at His trial, saying, "My kingdom is not of this world. If My kingdom were of this world, My servants would have been fighting, that I might not be delivered over to the Jews. But My kingdom is not from the world" (John 18:36). Jesus came to establish the kingdom of heaven, one which would last forever and institute a new life for those who believed in Him upon His death and resurrection. Even the mighty Roman Empire was feeble and tiny before the everlasting rule to which Jesus ascended, and He now sits at the right hand of God in all power and majesty.

He Will Tread Down Our Foes (Psalm 60)

During David's reign, he fought many battles. One such victory against Edom, perhaps the one mentioned in 2 Samuel 8:13–14, is the occasion of this psalm. David expresses two key emotions: first, when Israel suffers defeat in early battles, he feels rejected by God (vv. 1–8); then he feels confident in God's power to save (vv. 10–12). In the trials of life, we can feel confident that though we may feel rejected and abandoned, God has still saved us in Christ.

Lead Me to the Rock (Psalm 61)

Once again, David returns to the theme of asking God to restore him to the throne in Jerusalem. This likely happened during the time of Absalom's rebellion (2 Samuel 15–18), a period that occasioned many of David's psalms. Challenging times point us to our dependence on God, and here David uses some powerful images to relate his reliance on God's protection and preservation in all things.

CLEAR THE CONFUSION

What did David mean by "from the end of the earth I call to You when my heart is faint" (v. 2)?

When Absalom attempted his coup, David was forced to flee from Jerusalem and the temple and to escape over the Israelite border, as he once had to flee to Philistia when Saul had sought his life. David used the phrase "from the end of the earth I call to You" to express his isolation and loneliness so far from the temple in Jerusalem. His phrase "my heart is faint" shows David had exhausted his own courage, strength, and optimism. He was depressed, fearful, and tired. Unable to save himself, he called upon God for help.

When God feels distant and far away, when we feel helpless, defeated, and weary, we can pray these same words of David to Jesus Christ, our Lord and Savior.

LINK BETWEEN THE TESTAMENTS

Lead Me to the Rock → Build Your House on the Rock (Psalm 61 → Matthew 7:24–27)

Anyone in construction can tell you that foundations matter. It is not uncommon for the building of a foundation to take just as much time as the rest of a structure. Without a sure footing, the future of what is built on top of it is at best uncertain. The psalms often depict God as an immovable rock. Like a strong foundation to a building, rocks provide not only certainty in floods and bad weather but also a high ground that offers protection from enemies.

These themes continued into the New Testament when, for example, Jesus stated that those who hear His words and practice them are like a wise man who builds his home on a rock—a firm foundation. Throughout the Scriptures, God's Word is revealed and extolled as the only sure and firm basis for a secure future. The apostle Paul even went so far as to say that the foundation of the church and the foundation of the Christian life is Christ Himself, the solid rock (see 1 Corinthians 3:11). We who are built up in Him and His Word, by grace through faith, will be saved from the ancient enemy of death. We will also be able to firmly stand in this life as temptations and persecutions arise against God's people.

My Soul Waits for God Alone (Psalm 62)

The content of this psalm suggests that it was written late in David's life (perhaps around the time of 2 Samuel 23:1–7). In it, he reflects on the folly of bitterness, spite, envy, and betrayal that accompany the pursuit of wealth and power. He instead directs all God's people to trust in the Lord, as all salvation and glory come from Him.

CLEAR THE CONFUSION

What did David mean when he said, "Those of low estate are but a breath; those of high estate are a delusion; in the balances they go up; they are together lighter than a breath" (v. 9)?

Ancient balances were scales that had two pans. An object was placed in the right pan, which dropped down under the weight until another object was placed in the left pan. If that object was heavier than the first, the right pan went up.

Those of low estate are the poor and lower class, who are treated with contempt in most cultures. Those of high estate are the wealthy, prominent, successful people. David was saying that the poor and the rich can be placed together in one pan, and that pan will go up when the breath or Word of God is placed in the other.

This was David's way of saying the opinions and advice of both the poor and wealthy are absolutely meaningless. David only trusted in the Word or breath of God.

My Soul Thirsts for You (Psalm 63)

David's words in this psalm indicate that he may have been on the run or recalling a time when he was on the run at the time of its composition (perhaps again from Absalom). David feels far away from the Lord, fainting to be in His presence. Though he is far away and cut off from the temple, David still praises God, using the occasion as an opportunity to reflect upon his need for God's presence and deliverance.

Hide Me from the Wicked (Psalm 64)

David points out the smug arrogance of the wicked who plot against God's people, convinced that they have hidden their intentions, completely unaware that God knows their plots. David pleads for God to hide him and promises the believers that God will faithfully rescue them from those who pursue them and try to snare them. God will turn their wicked plots against them. God's people can rejoice in His faithful protection.

O God of Our Salvation (Psalm 65)

What words of thanks and praise from Psalm 65 can you incorporate into your own prayers on your own or in your household?

This psalm of praise covers the full breadth of what God's people thank Him for, and it would be perfect for a harvest festival. God has protected us, provided for us, and, most importantly, atoned for our transgressions. Today we can echo these praises as we go about our vocations as God's people and enjoy the bounties He provides for us, thanking Him for His mercy, grace, and provision for us.

CLEAR THE CONFUSION

What did David mean by "who stills the roaring of the seas, the roaring of their waves, the tumult of the peoples" (v. 7)?

David used three parallel phrases to describe war between nations. The noise of battle is similar to the roaring of the seas and waves crashing against one another. Just as God stills the storms on the sea, so He brings war to an end and establishes peace between nations.

How Awesome Are Your Deeds (Psalm 66)

As this psalm is not attributed to David, the content suggests that it may have been written at the time of Hezekiah, when the mighty Assyrian army surrounded Jerusalem (2 Kings 19:8–37). In it, the psalmist states how God brought trial upon His people yet delivered them from it. For any of God's people experiencing hardship today, we can still trust that God listens and attends to our prayers.

CLEAR THE CONFUSION

How was silver "tried" in the time of this psalmist?

In verse 10, the psalmist says, "For You, O God, have tested us; You have tried us as silver is tried." To refine silver and remove all the impurities, the silver had to be subjected to a very high temperature. But the silversmith had to carefully watch and control the heat. If the fire was not hot enough, the impurities would not be drawn out of the silver. If the fire was too hot, the silver would burn up.

When we go through a fiery trial in life (1 Peter 4:12), our God is watching and controlling everything very carefully. He allows the situation to exert enough pressure on us that it makes us abandon our sinful pride and self-confidence and flee to God for help. But He makes certain the situation isn't so overpowering that we despair and are driven away from Him.

How does the close attention of the silversmith during the smelting process give you comfort when you consider God's presence and His careful attention whenever you suffer through a fiery trial?

Make Your Face Shine upon Us (Psalm 67)

The opening lines of this short psalm suggest that it may have been written for the congregation of God's people to sing either immediately before or after the benediction God gave Aaron in Numbers 6:24–26, which we still use in worship today. Verse 6, praising God for His ongoing blessings of food and provision, shows this psalm may have been written on the occasion of a harvest. This psalm clearly shows God's desire for the salvation of all people and reminded Israel, just as it reminds us, that our mission is to share God's glory with all nations on earth.

God Shall Scatter His Enemies (Psalm 68)

Though it is not mentioned in the superscription, this psalm was likely written to be used in a worship procession. As the worshipers made their way to the tabernacle or temple, they recalled how God scattered the enemies of His people before them. In our worship, we, too, can praise God for His mighty deeds and recall His wondrous works.

VISUALIZE

CLEAR THE CONFUSION

What is meant by "The chariots of God are twice ten thousand, thousands upon thousands; the Lord is among them; Sinai is now in the sanctuary" (v. 17)?

The psalmist had been speaking of the exodus from Egypt and of God guiding Israel to Mount Sinai, where He made a covenant with Israel. The "chariots of God" are the angels who surround Him (see Ezekiel 10:1). "Sinai is now in the sanctuary" means God's glorious presence did not remain on Mount Sinai when Israel moved on toward the Promised Land. Rather, His glory filled the tabernacle (Exodus 40:34–38) and went with them every step of the way.

LINK BETWEEN THE TESTAMENTS

You Ascended on High → When He Ascended on High (Psalm 68:18 → Ephesians 4:8)

Paul used this verse from the psalm in Ephesians 4:8 to speak of Jesus' ascension forty days after His resurrection from the dead. He states that through Christ's victorious death, resurrection, and ascension, He led a host of captives free from Satan's power and gave gifts to mankind, those gifts being apostles, prophets, evangelists, pastors, and teachers to share the good news of God's mercy and forgiveness in Jesus Christ.

Save Me, O God (Psalm 69)

In this psalm, David pours out his prayer as he is attacked on all sides by the enemies of God's people. Even so, he praises God in the midst of these attacks. We who are attacked by the fallen powers of the devil, the world, and our sinful flesh can learn from David's prayer.

How are you being attacked by the powers of the devil, the world, or your sinful flesh right now? What can you learn about how to resist those ancient enemies from Psalm 69?

PICTURE OF THE SAVIOR

A Messianic Psalm

Psalm 69 is David's prayer for help as he suffers attacks from his enemies. Jesus, the Son of David, suffered even greater attacks and persecution as He took our sins to the cross. Several of the verses are quoted in the Gospels and fit very well with Jesus' Passion:

Verse 9: "Zeal for Your house has consumed me." (See John 2:17.)
Verse 21: "For my thirst they gave me sour wine to drink." (See Matthew 27:34.)

LINK BETWEEN THE TESTAMENTS

Save Me, O God → Paul's Thorn in the Flesh (Psalm 69 → 2 Corinthians 12:1–10)

Both Old and New Testament believers recognized that their weakness was a conduit through which God could work miraculous things and best show His preeminence. David sang Psalms 69 and 70 to praise God's power to rescue him and to reveal His might to those who would mock him, writing, "Let heaven and earth praise Him, the seas and everything that moves in them. For God will save Zion and build up the cities of Judah, and people shall dwell there and possess it" (Psalm 69:34–35).

In the same way, the apostle Paul would glorify God's ability to work with weakness. After telling the church in Corinth about the "thorn" God had given to him, Paul declared, "But He said to me, 'My grace is sufficient for you, for My power is made perfect in weakness.' Therefore I will boast all the more gladly of my weaknesses, so that the power of Christ may rest upon me" (2 Corinthians 12:9). For both of these men, God used their afflictions and weaknesses to display His greatness more prominently to the world. In fact, Jesus only achieved His victory through the ultimate weakness, humbling Himself to death on a cross so that we would no longer be weak in sin but be forever strengthened in Him.

O LORD, Do Not Delay (Psalm 70)

This psalm of David is described as being for the memorial offering, in which certain parts of an offering were especially set aside to the Lord (as in Leviticus 2:2). Here, David asks God to remember his neediness and poverty and to deliver him from those who attack him. Verse 1 is used at the beginning of the services of Matins and Vespers (*LSB*, pp. 219, 229).

LINK BETWEEN THE TESTAMENTS

"Let them turn back because of their shame who say, 'Aha, Aha!'" → "And those who passed by derided Him, wagging their heads and saying, 'Aha!'" (Psalm 70:3 → Mark 15:29)

In verse 3, David speaks of enemies who say, "Aha, Aha!" This expression is filled with malicious joy and derision as an evildoer celebrates the sufferings of a believer. David's enemies, especially people of Saul's tribe of Benjamin, misjudged calamities that fell upon David as proof that he had usurped the throne of Israel that rightly belonged to Saul and his descendants. (See 2 Samuel 16:5–8, in which Shimei of Benjamin curses David.)

On Good Friday, when Jesus hung on the cross, many of the Jews who passed by Him wagged their heads and said, "Aha! You who would destroy the temple and rebuild it in three days, save Yourself, and come down from the cross!" (Mark 15:29–30). It is as if they were saying, "You had us fooled on Sunday when we thought You were the Messiah, but we see clearly now. You are nothing but a fraud, a blasphemer, and a criminal."

CLEAR THE CONFUSION

What does "I am poor and needy" (v. 5) mean?

In the Scriptures, we often see the phrase "poor and needy." Sometimes it refers to those who are economically poor and struggling to meet their needs. But even though David went through times of poverty, he was also a wealthy king. In this and many other cases, this phrase is talking about spiritual poverty and neediness.

Because of our sinful nature, no matter what our bank accounts may show, every one of us is poor and needy before God. None of us have a wealth of goodness and purity with which to secure His assistance. We cannot keep ourselves alive. But God has given His dear Son, Jesus Christ, who became poor that we might become rich. He took our sin upon Himself and has clothed us in His righteousness, holiness, and perfection. "I am poor and needy" is a confession of our sin and a call for God to forgive us and restore us as His own children.

Forsake Me Not When My Strength Is Spent (Psalm 71)

Though not ascribed to David, this psalm was likely written by him in his old age. He returns to common themes found throughout the book of Psalms: refuge, assault, and salvation. Growing older does not automatically bring us closer to God, as many of the kings of David's line show in 2 Kings; many of them started close to God, then grew proud, complacent, or stubborn. May the limitations that come upon us in our later years drive us to repent of our sin and cling to God's Word. Throughout our lifespan, God's people are to constantly cling to the truths of God's Word and to declare those truths to our children and our children's children.

Compare the language and themes of Psalm 71 to other psalms of David. How has old age changed his perspective?

CLEAR THE CONFUSION

Why did the psalmist describe himself as "a portent to many" (v. 7)?

A *portent* is a sign. The psalmist meant that many looked upon the circumstances in his life and used those circumstances to wrongly judge his faith or God's opinion of him. When he succeeded or prospered, they took it as a sign that God was pleased with him. When he suffered or faced adversity, they took it as a portent that his faith was weak or that God was displeased with him. In this case, the difficulties attendant upon old age were convincing many that God was against him. The psalmist says that despite how circumstances may look, God is his strong refuge—and ours too.

Sadly, Jesus' disciples fell victim to this kind of judging when they saw a man who had been born blind and assumed either he or his parents had sinned (John 9:1–2). Jesus would likewise be misjudged on account of His crucifixion. May God guard us from mercilessly judging others that way.

Give the King Your Justice (Psalm 72)

This psalm notes a transition point in the book. It is "of Solomon," meaning it was either written by or for Solomon at his coronation. In addition, the final verse notes that there would be no more psalms written by David. Though some songs of David are found later in the book, the psalm notes that an era of songwriting has passed. The psalm asks for God's continued guidance and blessing on the kings in the line of David. Though some would be more faithful than others, all would be sinful and in need of salvation until the final king in the line of David, Christ, would appear. As you read this psalm, think of the blessings of Christ's rule: how it endures forever and offers forgiveness, salvation, peace, and eternal life to all people of all nations to the ends of the earth.

VISUALIZE

LINK BETWEEN THE TESTAMENTS

May the Kings Bring Gifts → The Wise Men Bring Their Gifts to Jesus (Psalm 72:10 → Matthew 2:1–12)

Many kings and queens heard of Solomon's wisdom and came with great gifts to meet him. When Jesus was born, Wise Men from the East came to worship Him and present their gifts to Him.

Book Three, Mostly Nationalistic Psalms of Asaph and the Sons of Korah (Psalms 73–89)

Whereas Books One and Two of the Psalms prominently feature psalms written either by David or at the time of David, Book Three shifts to psalms written later in Israel's history. Many of these are ascribed to Asaph, a Levite whom David appointed as one of the tabernacle song leaders. Ascribing these psalms to Asaph does not mean Asaph wrote each one. More likely, they were written by a later descendant from Asaph's family line. As you read through and meditate on Book Three, pay attention to the historical cues given in many of the summaries in this guide. They will help you nest the psalm in the most likely historical context that was the occasion for writing the psalm.

God Is My Strength and Portion Forever (Psalm 73)

WAYPOINT

What prosperity traps named in this psalm stand out to you the most? Why?

What does this text show us?
In this psalm, the psalmist wrestles with feelings of envy toward evildoers who are prosperous in life. Why do they seem to have so much success and happiness in life, when he has dedicated himself to serving the Lord faithfully? Even so, in the end, the seeming success of the wicked is fleeting, and they will perish. Instead of following the way of the world, the psalmist concludes, we should seek to be near God and follow His guidance. His salvation is forever.

How did Christ demonstrate for us godly priorities and purpose in life?

What does this text reveal about God's plan of salvation?
The main theme of this psalm reflects a main theme in the book of Job: Why do the wicked seem to prosper while the righteous suffer? This theme appears not only in Job and other sections of the Scriptures but also in life. Why does it seem like bad things happen to good people while bad people get away with so much wickedness? This psalm answers the question with the reality that all earthly success, though it seems so important at the time, means nothing in eternity. On the cross, Christ overcame the world for us. Though all things pass away, those who are in Christ and His forgiveness will remain forever.

What is one way you can better prioritize God's Word over the things of the world in your life right now?

What does this text uncover about our identity and calling as God's people today?
Life is a constant fight against envy. We are tempted on all sides, especially in the age of advertisements, social media, and digital marketing, to break the Ninth and Tenth Commandments. We want what others have, be it relationships

or possessions, and we are discontented with what God has chosen to give us. God's people are to be ever vigilant against these temptations. In reality, in Christ, we have been given the greatest treasure of all time. We have been given eternal life and a new eternal identity in Christ. As we navigate this world, tempted to covet so much, we can take comfort in the psalmist's words and be content with the good things God has given out of His fatherly love.

Arise, O God, Defend Your Cause (Psalm 74)

Verse 3 of this psalm suggests that it was written after the destruction of the Jerusalem temple by the Babylonians in 587 BC. Furthermore, the mention in verse 9 that there is not any prophet hints that it was composed after Jeremiah was taken to Egypt (Jeremiah 43). This means the "Of Asaph" superscription at the beginning points to a descendant of Asaph as the composer. In the calamities of life, when all hope seems lost, we can follow the psalmist's lead and remember God's faithfulness to His people in the past and promises of salvation to us in the future.

How can the words of Psalm 74 give you strength in times of calamity and loss?

God Will Judge with Equity (Psalm 75)

As we saw in Psalm 74, the context of this psalm hints at it being written later in the period of God's people, likely when the kingdom of Judah was under attack by unbelieving foes (as in 2 Kings 18–19). From verse 2 through verse 4, the psalmist uses first-person perspective as God speaks His judgments on the wicked. God delivers His people in His time, not ours, but as we wait, we can trust in God's promises to never leave us or forsake us. These promises will finally be fulfilled in Christ.

CLEAR THE CONFUSION

What is the cup of God's judgment?

Psalm 75:8 includes a metaphor for God's wrath that, though it is somewhat common in the Bible, seems strange to our modern ears. In this metaphor, God's wrath is like a cup of strong drink that He hands to the wicked, who then drink this cup and experience God's judgment. This image appears in the Old Testament prophets in Isaiah 51:22; Jeremiah 25:15; and Obadiah 16. The image is a powerful one: when people foolishly drink too much alcohol, they bring upon themselves drunkenness and shame. They go about staggering and falling. God's wrath is like a cup that foolish people drink of and, through their own foolish choices and actions, bring destruction upon themselves. Though it is God's wrath, and it is His will to pass along that wrath because of sin, it is the sinful choices of the wicked that bring about self-harm and self-destruction.

This Old Testament theme is ultimately fulfilled by Christ. Before going to the cross, Jesus prayed that the Father would take the cup of God's wrath from Him, but He accepted that it was God's will that He consume the cup (Luke 22:42). Jesus, on the cross, took from sinful humanity the cup of God's wrath that we all deserve to drink and consumed it Himself in our place. In His death on the cross, He absorbed into Himself the whole of humanity's judgment, offering Himself in our place. We who believe in Christ are now freed from God's wrath as He took the cup for us, fulfilling the Old Testament Law in our stead. Instead of the cup of wrath, He offers us the cup of blessing, His own blood to drink in Holy Communion.

Who Can Stand Before You? (Psalm 76)

Context clues from Psalms 76 and 77 suggest that they were both written in the later stages of the Old Testament. How is the historical context of these psalms reflected in the words or phrases chosen by the author?

In light of contextual cues in verses 5, 6, and 12, the occasion of this psalm was likely the deliverance of God's people from the invading forces of the Assyrians during the reign of Hezekiah (Isaiah 36–37). God sent an angel who destroyed 185,000 Assyrian warriors, single-handedly defeating a grand army of the world's most feared expanding empire to save His people. God's power is greater than that of any kings of the earth, and He chooses to save His people, granting them forgiveness and life.

CLEAR THE CONFUSION

What is "Salem" (v. 2)?

The word *Salem* means "peace." It is a form of the word *Shalom*, meaning peace, greetings, or the like. It is also part of the longer city name *Jeru-Salem*, which means "City of Peace." The psalmist used it here as a nickname for Jerusalem in a way that emphasizes the peace God gives in this city through the temple.

What is meant by "Surely the wrath of man shall praise You" (v. 10)?

This phrase can be understood in a couple of ways. One is that all evildoers will praise God and acknowledge His authority when they stand before Christ's judgment seat being condemned by Him. Another way to understand it is to say that God will glorify Himself when He protects His people from the wrath of sinful people who try to destroy them. If this psalm is indeed praising God for delivering Jerusalem from the Assyrians, then God certainly received praise because He miraculously stopped the Assyrians who had come in a rage to destroy Jerusalem.

In the Day of Trouble I Seek the Lord (Psalm 77)

Similarities between themes in this psalm and those in the book of Habakkuk suggest that it was composed around the time of Habakkuk (that is, around 605 BC). In this psalm, the psalmist instructs God's people on what to do when they are overwhelmed with anxiety from troubling circumstances and are struggling with faith, wondering if God has forsaken them forever. They are to meditate on God's wonderful deeds of old—against seemingly impossible odds, God brought Israel out of Egypt and through the waters of the Red Sea after decades of slavery. The psalmist urges us to remember God's faithfulness and wait for Him to finally fulfill His promises.

VISUALIZE

"I will remember the deeds of the Lord." (Psalm 77:11)

PICTURE OF THE SAVIOR

Strength by the Word

The psalmist's chief reminder in Psalm 77 crystallizes the strengthening power of God's Word for downtrodden believers. When we are beset by troubles, weariness, or loneliness, he exhorts us to recall the great works of God and rest in the sure promises they offer. For Israel, their rescue from physical slavery in Egypt fortified their resolve and gave them peace in gloomy times. God revealed His faithfulness to them in their delivery to the Promised Land through Moses.

As the Word made flesh, Jesus is the greatest of these works and gives the best reminder of God's faithfulness through the Gospel. He rescued us from spiritual slavery to sin and redeemed us by His blood, counting us forevermore righteous and heirs to His kingdom. In this advice to fellow believers, the writer shows how Jesus, God's living Word, strengthens us by His promise and act of salvation in the cross and empty tomb.

Tell the Coming Generation (Psalm 78)

Sometimes called the teaching psalm, Psalm 78 was written at a time after the construction of the temple under Solomon. The psalmist instructs the people to look at God's gracious works in the past and to not be like the generation of Israelites who grumbled against God and disobeyed Him in the wilderness after leaving Egypt or like the Israelites who turned to idolatry after God had brought them into the Promised Land. The psalm ends by pointing to God's covenant with David (2 Samuel 7:1–17). Christians today can look back at God's faithfulness, especially His faithfulness in sending Christ, the descendant of David, for the sins of the world.

?

What can Christians today learn from Psalm 78 about the importance and methods of passing on the faith to the next generation?

VISUALIZE

Israel passes through the Red Sea.

CLEAR THE CONFUSION

What are the "dark sayings" (v. 2)?

Dark sayings are not sayings that are evil but sayings that are mysterious or hidden because they must be discerned through the Holy Spirit and faith. Jesus spoke in parables, which could only be understood through faith; their spiritual meaning remained hidden to the unbelieving Jews who thought they had to earn heaven by their good works.

What is the phrase "The Ephraimites, armed with the bow, turned back on the day of battle" (v. 9) speaking about?

In Numbers 14, after hearing the evil report of the ten unbelieving spies, the people of Israel (often represented by the tribe of Ephraim) grumbled against Moses and Aaron and refused to enter the Promised Land to take possession of it. As the psalmist says, they forgot the mighty works of God (recorded in Exodus 13–17 and Numbers 11) that should have given them confidence He would defeat the Canaanites for them.

What is the "dwelling at Shiloh" that God rejected (v. 60)?

This event is recorded in 1 Samuel 4. When the Israelites settled in Canaan, the tabernacle was set up in Shiloh. Because of Israel's idolatry, God raised up the Philistines against them, and the Philistines captured the ark of the covenant and destroyed the town of Shiloh. The tabernacle was moved to Gibeon, where it remained until Solomon built the Jerusalem temple and brought the tabernacle into it (1 Kings 8:4).

What does "and delivered His power to captivity, His glory to the hand of the foe" (v. 61) mean?

This refers to the ark of the covenant, which the Philistines captured from the faithless Israelites, as recorded in 1 Samuel 4. Verses 65–66 describe God's punishment of the Philistines (see 1 Samuel 5–6), which drove them to return the ark to Israel.

SET THE SCENE

Oral Tradition and History

Psalm 78 highlights the oral nature of ancient cultures. As many people were illiterate and technology for copying manuscripts was minimal, oral tradition was the primary path of passing along wisdom from generation to generation. Unless they faithfully passed on the stories of old, future generations would be deprived of knowing of God's mighty deeds. Though we live in a much more literate world today and technology has never been more prevalent, we dare not miss the importance of the oral tradition. As the psalmist prompts in Psalm 78, we, too, are to pass along the wisdom of God's Word from generation to generation, talking about God's mighty deeds openly and boldly with one another in the community of the church so that the younger generations may learn from our words and example.

How Long, O LORD? (Psalm 79)

The context of this psalm implies that it was written sometime during the Babylonian exile following the destruction of Jerusalem in 587 BC. The psalmist laments how unbelievers have defiled the temple. On one hand, the psalm asks for God's forgiveness, as the sins of Judah had led to the ultimate destruction of Jerusalem. On the other hand, the psalmist calls upon God's promises, trusting that God will not let the Babylonians' evil works go unchecked forever. This psalm is a perfect prayer for Christians undergoing persecution from unbelievers.

Restore Us, O God (Psalm 80)

The writing of this curious psalm may have been prompted by refugees from the Northern Kingdom of Israel who were seeking asylum in the Southern Kingdom of Judah when their kingdom fell to the Assyrian invasion (2 Kings 17), around 722 BC. The psalm is a prayer for God to restore His people after their conquest by foreigners. Christians know that our prayer for restoration is heard and fulfilled by Christ.

Oh, That My People Would Listen to Me (Psalm 81)

This psalm has no date, but the context implies it might have been written for use in tabernacle worship. The psalmist uses first-person narrative to express God's desire for His people to listen to Him and walk in His way. It recounts the attitudes of God's people, both positive and negative, as they left Egypt after the exodus. It is a call to listen to and not ignore God's Word, because God wants to bless our lives richly in Jesus and wants to guard us from the unnecessary suffering we bring on ourselves by our sins.

LINK BETWEEN THE TESTAMENTS

Listen to God's Calling → The Bread of Life (Psalm 81 → John 6:22–59)

It may be easy for us as we read the accounts of wilderness wanderings in the Books of Moses to miss just how monumental the gift of manna was to God's people. Think about it. Every day (but the Sabbath) God's people would wake up and gather the miraculous breadlike substance that came from heaven during the night. Every day. For forty years. This daily bread from heaven, alluded to in Psalm 81:16, foreshadowed the true bread from heaven, Jesus, who came from heaven to give eternal life to all who believe in Him. This Jesus, the Word of God made flesh, sustains us in our journey though this life and into the next.

Rescue the Weak and Needy (Psalm 82)

Whom has God put in authority over you in your life? How can Psalm 82 serve as a model for how to properly pray for them?

This psalm uses language of divine counsel to remind us that God holds all earthly leaders accountable for how they fulfill the heavy responsibilities He gives them, both in the church and in the state. God judges each of them for their faithlessness. This is a reminder for all us of to pray for our leaders and, in whatever capacity we lead our families, churches, or communities, to repent and receive forgiveness from God that we might be a blessing to those people God has committed to our care and leadership.

CLEAR THE CONFUSION

Why did the psalmist call God-ordained authorities "gods" (v. 6)?

This psalm may prompt readers to do a double take. Who are the gods mentioned here? Jesus Himself clarified in John 10:34 that the "gods" mentioned in the psalm are those people to whom the Word of God came. Specifically, in this psalm, they are the leaders and judges of God's people on earth who have received the commission to lead and speak God's Word to the assembly. All believers in Jesus are made children of God and are therefore God's representatives in this world. We who have been baptized have been marked with the very triune name of God Himself (Matthew 28:19). This is a marvelous blessing! By faith, our lives are now one with Christ (Galatians 2:20). As God's children, and as His representatives here on earth, we are called to avoid the sins and errors named in Psalm 82:2 and instead to faithfully proclaim His Word and live out His will in our lives that more may come to a saving faith in Christ.

O God, Do Not Keep Silence (Psalm 83)

Context clues from this psalm mark its writing as likely between the time of Solomon's death and the Assyrian invasion of the kingdom of Israel, roughly between 931 and 722 BC. In it, the psalmist lists a long chain of enemy neighbors who surround and constantly threaten God's people (vv. 6–8). Yet the psalm also includes a list of historical victories during the time of the judges (vv. 9–12). The psalm ends with a call for God to remove the enemies of His people from their presence and bring them to shame, thus bringing honor to God's name.

?

If you had to rephrase the main theme of Psalm 83 in your own words, how would you express it? Why would you phrase it that way?

My Soul Longs for the Courts of the LORD (Psalm 84)

This psalm, written by the descendants of Korah, was likely written after the temple was completed. The psalmist takes the perspective of one who is separated from being able to worship with the community, longing for the day when he or she will be able to gather in corporate worship in God's presence. What a great reminder for us today not only to gather with others in worship to receive God's gifts but also to remember and serve those who are unable to regularly attend with us.

CLEAR THE CONFUSION

What is the "Valley of Baca" (v. 6)?

The Hebrew word *Baca* means "tears." We don't know if this was an actual location or a figurative one like the "valley of the shadow of death" in Psalm 23:4. In either case, the psalmist is reminding us that when we are going through times of pain, loss, and suffering, we find joy and strength from our fellow Christians, who comfort us by reminding us of God's steadfast love and mercy.

SET THE SCENE

The Blessing of Corporate Worship

Psalm 84 serves as a reminder of the great blessing we have in worship. In our day and age, with so many easy excuses not to attend corporate worship with other believers, it's easy to make worship attendance optional. But looking at the text of this psalm, along with so many other Scriptures, we see that God's desire is that we yearn for times of gathering around God's Word together, receiving His gifts. Yes, there may be times when we are apart, but these should be the exception and not the rule. Instead, we are to follow God's command, as the Israelites did in the tabernacle and temple worship, and take every opportunity we have to gather together with God's people around God's gifts.

Revive Us Again (Psalm 85)

The context of this psalm suggests it was written soon after the arrival of God's people back to the Promised Land after the exile in Babylon, around 538 BC. The psalmist both praises God for returning the people and asks for God's ongoing restoration of His people amid the opposition of unbelievers and the uncertainties of life. Christians today can learn from this how to thank God for His faithfulness to us in Christ and to ask God for ongoing protection from the fallen powers that constantly assail us.

Great Is Your Steadfast Love (Psalm 86)

This psalm surprisingly is attributed to David, his only psalm in Book Three. It reads like a personal prayer of David asking for God to hear him, preserve him, gladden him, forgive him, and teach him. This serves as a powerful prayer model for Christians for all time.

CLEAR THE CONFUSION

What does the phrase "to You, O Lord, do I lift up my soul" (v. 4) mean?

This is a cry of deep distress, a calling out to God for help. It asks Him to search our heart and soul and to see our desperate need for forgiveness, help, and peace. This phrase is recited in one of our Communion liturgies and carries the same sense. We are poor, miserable sinners who need our Savior to come to us in His body and blood and save us.

What is meant by "unite my heart to fear Your name" (v. 11)?

In this earthly life, we believers are saints and sinners at the same time. Because of that, our hearts are divided with competing loyalties between God and our selfish desires for things we make gods in our lives. This phrase is a plea to God to cleanse our hearts of these sinful desires so we may truly fear, love, and trust in Him above all gods.

What are "the depths of Sheol" (v. 13)?

In this case, Sheol is not hell but death and the grave. This is a thanksgiving to God for sparing David's life that he may continue to serve God here on earth.

PICTURE OF THE SAVIOR

The One Who Answers in Love

In this noteworthy psalm, David highlighted the defining feature of the true God—His steadfast love—and outlined the manner in which Christ would embody that attribute to the fullest. False gods worshiped by nations hostile to Israel were thought of as being very transactional in their dealings with lowly humans. Worship often involved placating their wrath or beseeching them to do something by offering one or multiple acts of devotion. Only once the "bill was paid" with gift or deed offerings would the false gods bless the people with what they needed or desired. In a reversal of expectations, the true God descended to His people, humbling Himself to the point of becoming man. There were no requirements met, no standards achieved by Israel; in fact, they had turned away from Him time and time again. Instead, Jesus Christ offered Himself up to the ruthless men who sought His life as a willing sacrifice to die and win victory over death itself.

Glorious Things of You Are Spoken (Psalm 87)

This short psalm provides a window into God's epic plan of salvation for the nations through His Bride, the church. In verse 4, believing Gentiles are mentioned. Though they were not born in Zion, through faith they can be counted among God's people who were. What a marvelous song of the power of God to make all who believe in Him His children by faith in the promise of Christ! Jesus will use this imagery of being born into God's family to teach about Baptism. Hymn writer John Newton based his hymn text "Glorious Things of You Are Spoken" (*LSB* 648) on this psalm.

Taking cues from Psalm 87, whom can you identify as unbelievers in your community whom you can pray for today? Pray not only that they would come to faith but also that God would provide opportunities for you to share the Gospel with them.

I Cry Out Day and Night Before You (Psalm 88)

The unique author of (or dedication to) this psalm is Heman the Ezrahite, who was possibly the descendant of Zerah, son of Judah and grandson of Jacob (1 Chronicles 2:6). The psalmist is overcome with sadness and loneliness, feelings common to the broken human experience. Yet the psalmist in his brokenness cries out to the Lord, an action we are to emulate in our feelings of abandonment. The expressions of the author could well fit our Savior's sufferings, loneliness, and abandonment on the cross.

I Will Sing of the Steadfast Love of the LORD (Psalm 89)

Similar to Psalm 88, this psalm is (most likely) dedicated to the descendant of Zerah named Ethan (1 Chronicles 2:6). It presents the rise and fall of the reign of David's family in epic scope, meaning it was likely written sometime after his death. It points to both the sins of David and the unfaithfulness of his descendants who ruled after him, as well as the sins of God's people. But it also recalls God's promise to David that one of his descendants would sit on the throne forever. Though the situation in Judah may have felt bleak and faithless at the time of this psalm, we know that the promise was ultimately fulfilled in Jesus, who lives and reigns forever.

VISUALIZE

CLEAR THE CONFUSION

Are sorrowful psalms a good thing?

There's a common misconception that Christians are supposed to be happy all the time. After all, we have the gift of salvation, so why not? The reality remains, however, that we still live in a broken world. There will be a day when the Lord Jesus, King of kings, returns in glory to destroy the power of death forever and to make all things new. We hope in this promise. But that promise is not yet fulfilled. Until then, we still struggle with the effects of death, the weakness of the flesh, and the demonic attacks of all that Satan can throw at God's people. The psalms encapsulate the life of God's people for all times and all places, including the joys and sorrows of living in this vale of tears. We learn from the sorrowful psalms how to properly grieve and that it's okay to be frustrated with the broken world. We also learn how to look to God's promises and God's character for hope for the future.

Book Four, Mostly Anonymous Psalms and Laments (Psalms 90–106)

Book Four of the Psalms turns away from the more nationalistic psalms of God's people in Israel to a more general set of songs and laments.

From Everlasting to Everlasting (Psalm 90)

There's no historical event named within this psalm. It is unique in that it is the only psalm attributed to Moses, which makes it possibly the most ancient of recorded psalms. The psalmist puts the lament of time into perspective. Though all of us sinful humans experience our frailty and see that all things pass away, God's eternal glory and power never change, and His grace and favor do not pass away either. As we live each day as God's children in Christ, we should keep the finality of life and our coming resurrection always in view, remembering God is our shelter and will always be there for us.

What are some connections between Psalm 90 and events in the life of God's people during the exodus? How does this psalm help further illuminate God's epic plan of salvation for them?

CLEAR THE CONFUSION

What does the phrase "from everlasting to everlasting You are God" (v. 2) tell us about God?

The phrase "from everlasting" looks backward in time before creation and sees God is there. "To everlasting" looks forward past Judgment Day, and God is there forever. Revelation 1:4 puts it another way to refer to God the Father: "Grace to you and peace from Him who is and who was and who is to come."

Why did Moses ask God to "teach us to number our days that we may get a heart of wisdom" (v. 12)?

Moses asked God to make us aware of how brief our earthly life really is. Then in that knowledge, we will not focus on the present but instead be mindful of how transient and changeable this life is so that we will cherish the eternal treasures God offers us through faith and will look forward to our Lord's return far more than whatever earthly pleasures we may be anticipating in our future in this life. This leads to repentance and faith that Jesus has conquered death and promises us everlasting life.

How does knowing that Satan sought to use Psalm 91 to tempt Jesus to sin change your view of this psalm? How does the rest of the psalm illuminate the event of Jesus' temptation?

My Refuge and My Fortress (Psalm 91)

In this anonymous psalm, the writer confesses his faith and trust that God is able to preserve and protect his life from danger. Satan later quoted part of this psalm in the wilderness in an attempt to get Jesus to abuse His divine power (Luke 4:9–12). To this temptation, Jesus responded that we are not to put the Lord to the test. This is a great rule for us too. We trust that God is able to preserve our life from all danger, but we are not to allow the experience of pain to tempt us to doubt God's goodness.

CLEAR THE CONFUSION

What is "the snare of the fowler" (v. 3)?

When someone wanted to catch a bird, he laid a snare or trap on the ground and used seed to lure the bird. When the bird hit the trip cord, the trap would suddenly capture it so the bird could not escape death. In this psalm, the fowler is an enemy who seeks to harm or kill us and lays a trap for us of which we are completely unaware.

How Great Are Your Works (Psalm 92)

This anonymous psalm is tied especially to the Sabbath. In ancient Israel, God commanded that no work would be done on the Sabbath (Saturday). Thus, as the psalm indicates, the Sabbath would be devoted to praise of God and meditation on His works. Though Christians are freed from this ceremonial obligation, we are commanded not to neglect gathering in worship to receive His Word and Sacraments.

CLEAR THE CONFUSION

Why are the righteous compared to cedars and palm trees?

Though strange to our modern ears, within the book of Psalms (and the entire Bible), this analogy makes sense. In Psalm 1, the psalmist compared a righteous person to a tree planted by water. This water is God's Word, and as we receive its gifts and meditate on it, we not only grow strong and secure but also bear fruit of good works. Like a strong and solid tree, our faith remains firm in the troubles and turmoils of life. Later in the Scriptures, Jesus extended this agricultural metaphor to Himself, the very Word of God made flesh. As He is the vine and we are the branches, we who abide in His Word for life not only will remain in the faith for eternal life but also will bear good fruit that will last (John 15).

THE LORD REIGNS (PSALM 93)

Psalm 93 may have been composed as part of the celebration of the Feast of Booths, when Israel remembered the forty years of wandering in the wilderness after leaving Egypt. The psalmist points out how God is mightier than the forces of nature and the crashing seas. Jesus demonstrated this powerfully in His miracles here on earth. He who stilled storms and walked across the Sea of Galilee rules all things in His creation. Even when disaster strikes, we can trust and hope in Him.

VISUALIZE

The LORD Will Not Forsake His People (Psalm 94)

This psalm appears to be part of a series of psalms (93 through 99) that focus on how God reigns as King over all things. Yet the series begins in this psalm with a cry for God to rise up and judge injustice in the world. As Christians, we live in the tension of now and not yet. Though Christ reigns now over all things, we often see evil seem to prevail. His glorious reign will not be visible and complete until He returns to raise the dead. Until then, we can both trust in God's power and cry out for justice against wickedness.

CLEAR THE CONFUSION

What does it mean to call the Lord a "God of vengeance" (v. 1)?

Vengeance is often demeaned in our culture, and we Christians are commanded by Christ to forgive those who do wrong against us. So why is God called a God of vengeance? It may seem beneath God to take vengeance against wrongs. But God hates evil and will not permit evil done against His loved ones to go unpunished. Good Friday is the clearest evidence of God's vengeance, when He punished Jesus for the sins of the world. When we are wronged, we forgive those who sin against us, asking God to bring them to repentance and salvation. But we leave it to God to vindicate us and avenge us on Judgment Day if those who sinned against us refuse to repent.

Let Us Sing Songs of Praise (Psalm 95)

The context of this psalm may put it as one of the songs used for the Feast of Booths. The psalmist directs the congregation of God's people to follow him in a great many prayers and praises and to remember God's mighty deeds of old. Verses 8–11 speak of Israel's grumbling, complaining, testing, and sinning during the forty years of wilderness wandering, making it perfect for the Feast of Booths, which commemorated God's loving providence and patience throughout those years.

SET THE SCENE

Psalms in Worship Services

Psalms continue to play an important role in corporate worship in many congregations across the world. Even if the psalms themselves aren't fully spoken or chanted, certain sections have been incorporated into various liturgies throughout time. In services such as the Divine Service, Matins, and

Vespers, psalms are generally used in word and song, notably in sections like the Introit, the Venite, the Jubilate, and the post-Communion canticle. The next time you are in a worship service, pay special attention to the order of worship, identifying those places that have been directly pulled or adapted from the Psalms for use in the congregation.

What are some phrases or ideas from these psalms of praise that you can use in your own prayer life?

Worship in the Splendor of Holiness (Psalm 96)

Psalm 96 is used two times in the Scriptures: first, in 1 Chronicles 16:23–34, David sings this psalm as he brings the ark of the covenant to Jerusalem; second, in the Greek translation of the Old Testament called the Septuagint, this psalm is ascribed to the time when the temple was rebuilt after the Babylonian captivity. This was likely added as an occasion for its use again later on. What a wonderful song of praise for God's ongoing faithfulness and mercy toward His people throughout their history! Its final verses speak of Christ's return on Judgment Day to remove the curse from creation (that is, sin and evil from the world) and to establish His eternal kingdom in the new heavens and the new earth forevermore.

The LORD Reigns (Psalm 97)

Continuing on in the series of psalms praising God's reign as King of kings, Psalm 97 takes a slightly different approach. In it, God's righteous reign involves judgment on idolatry and idolaters. The God who created the heavens and the earth and reigns over all is a jealous God and demonstrates His power over those who worship false gods.

Make a Joyful Noise to the LORD (Psalm 98)

This psalm greatly resembles Psalm 96. Making no mentions of sinners or false gods, the psalmist and those who repeat this psalm focus on the Lord alone, praising Him for His mighty acts and for His power over all creation. Notice the salvation God's right hand (Jesus) works for Him, a salvation that is for all peoples of all nations. Notice also the promise that the Lord will come to judge the earth. No wonder the seas, the world, the rivers, and the hills clap their hands and sing for joy together as Christ returns to restore creation forever.

The LORD Our God Is Holy (Psalm 99)

In this final of a series of psalms that focus on the holy reign of God as King of His creation (93 through 99), we hear the psalmist recalling

God's presence among His people both in the temple and in history. Through the pillar of cloud, God spoke to Moses, Aaron, and Samuel; through His presence over the ark of the covenant, He came to dwell as the center of worship. In Christ, God once and for all took on human flesh and made His permanent dwelling among humanity.

His Steadfast Love Endures Forever (Psalm 100)

Psalm 100 is a joyful doxology, or song of praise to God. Though it is short, it has been the inspiration for many other simple songs of praise to God throughout the millennia. It calls on us to joyfully gather together in God's presence to receive His gifts through His Word and Sacraments.

How can you incorporate the words of Psalm 100 into your own devotional life or that of your household?

I Will Walk with Integrity (Psalm 101)

The context of this psalm, ascribed to David, seems to be that of either a new king's coronation or the annual celebration of the anniversary of a king's reign. It consists of a set of promises a truly righteous king would make and enact to be faithful to God and His Law. This psalm reveals the responsibilities of Israel's king to enforce good citizenship. Finally, reread this psalm thinking of Jesus as this faithful King.

PICTURE OF THE SAVIOR

Christ Walks in Integrity

The royal promises outlined in Psalm 101 are lofty goals fit for only the greatest kings of the world to uphold, yet they accurately describe only one King in particular: Jesus Christ. As the likely author of this poem, David sought to pledge himself to upright leadership and honorable dealings with his people. He was most certainly the greatest king of the nation of Israel, bringing glory to God's name and prosperity to the people over whom God had placed him. Yet in the midst of all his accomplishments and adherence to God's will for his reign, David's sins with Bathsheba barred him from ever attaining this incredible standard. Many years after Israel's greatest days, a son of David would be born and live such a life of integrity. Jesus took His blameless blood and spilled it for our sake upon the cross so that we should be called blameless and live in eternity as a part of His kingdom.

Do Not Hide Your Face from Me (Psalm 102)

In this psalm of repentance, we are given no specific reason for the psalmist's agony. Instead, we see the depth of the physical, spiritual, emotional, and social discomfort and unrest his sin and guilt are causing him. He feels weary and drained. Even so, the psalmist prays for God's forgiveness.

CLEAR THE CONFUSION

What did the psalmist mean when he said, "My days are like an evening shadow" (v. 11)?

As sunset approaches, shadows lengthen until the sun disappears—and with it the shadow. The psalmist is saying his life is nearing its end, an idea further reflected in the second half of that verse, which reads, "I wither away like grass."

How can we faithfully respond, in our times of despair, when people say, "God has a plan for you"?

Especially among Christians, we often don't know how to respond when people experience hardship, disappointment, suffering, anguish, loss, or pain. A common refrain many give to those who suffer is "God has a plan for you." To those experiencing this suffering, however, these words can easily bring feelings of confusion or anger. After all, are we to believe that God brings about evil in our lives and that we are to simply accept evil as part of God's will? Can't we call evil *evil* and good *good*? Popular Bible verses such as Jeremiah 29:11 and Romans 8:28 do indicate that God can work good out of evil, and in the end, God overcomes sin, death, and hell in Christ. But unless Christ returns in our lifetime, we will not see that final victory during our life.

Psalm 102 provides a wonderful example of how we are to respond to hardship and evil. First, we are to confess our sins, trusting that even if our suffering is not a direct consequence of our actions, we all need repentance. In our suffering, we see clearly the cross of Christ, why He came, and the wonderful gift of forgiveness that He gives. God redeemed the world through Christ's suffering, and in our suffering, we can thank God for what Jesus went through to redeem us. Second, we are to trust that God is still faithful to us, even if we do not know why this or that particular evil happens to us. We may never know why, and it is not for us to speculate. Instead, we can trust that God is able to, and does, salvage this broken world to His ends. Like the psalmist, we can trust that in the end future generations will know God's blessings—even when we experience hardship—and we can look to Him in all trials.

Bless the LORD, O My Soul (Psalm 103)

Just as Psalms 93–99 were united by the theme of the glorious reign of God, so Psalms 103–106 constitute a series united by their calls to praise the Lord. This one, of David, includes many memorable phrases that have been used within the community of God's people for centuries.

As you read through Psalms 103–106, pay special attention to how the psalmists praise God. How can these psalms serve as examples for you in your prayers and devotion times?

LINK BETWEEN THE TESTAMENTS

Bless the Lord → The Magnificat (Psalm 103 → Luke 1:46–55)

There are many Spirit-inspired "golden threads" throughout the Bible. These are ongoing, repeated themes. One powerful example is the theme of God bringing down the mighty and raising up the lowly out of His mercy and grace. This theme was memorably expressed in the song of Hannah (1 Samuel 2) and mirrored in Mary's hymn of praise at the announcement of Jesus' conception and birth by the angel Gabriel (Luke 1). Yet these are not the only two places where this is expounded upon. Here in Psalm 103 and in following psalms, David also understood this mysterious grace of God, praising God for His forgiveness and mercy. In God, we, who are lowly and deserve nothing because of our sin, are brought up from the pit of sin and death and given God's everlasting covenant. As we read the Scriptures and joyously marvel at God's words and ways, we can continue to look for this ongoing theme.

O LORD My God, You Are Very Great (Psalm 104)

Psalm 104 became part of the temple worship of God's people, likely used as part of the new year celebration. It paints a sweeping epic depiction of God ruling over creation, bringing to mind the first chapter of Genesis. Though we are to primarily see God through His revealed Word, we can also marvel at His creation and praise Him for what He has made, as the psalmist does.

LINK BETWEEN THE TESTAMENTS

The Greatness of the Lord → The Preeminence of Christ (Psalm 104 → Colossians 1:15–26)

Psalm 104 describes God's splendor as the ingenious Creator of all things. With much more language of praise, the psalmist describes God's creative project on the first six days as an extension of His glory. He notes God's intricate design and lauds the special care and attention that He continues to give today. In his closing words, the psalmist prays that all who desecrate the wonders that God has created would be destroyed, thus revealing the immense value of the gift of creation.

When writing to the Colossians, Paul similarly implored the church to be good stewards of the things God has given us: "of which I became a minister according to the stewardship from God that was given to me for you, to make the word of God fully known, the mystery hidden for ages and generations but now revealed to His saints" (Colossians 1:25–26). God has called us to be stewards of His creation from the beginning in Adam and Eve, caring for and honoring all that He has created for our benefit. Furthermore, as Paul speaks to us here, we are to be stewards of the Gospel, the Good News, which has redeemed the missteps of Adam and Eve and all sin ever since through Christ's death and resurrection. God has graciously given us much; we can honor Him in big ways by how we treat His gifts.

CLEAR THE CONFUSION

What was God's rebuke, "the sound of Your thunder" (v. 7)?

It was God's command "Let the waters under the heavens be gathered together into one place, and let the dry land appear" in Genesis 1:9. Notice the way the psalmist portrayed the enormous power of God's spoken word. Jesus used that same power and authority when He told the winds and waves on the Sea of Galilee, "Peace! Be still!" (Mark 4:39).

How do Psalms 105–107 work together to tell one cohesive story? How are they different?

Tell of All His Wonderful Works (Psalm 105)

Psalms 105–107, combined, recall the narrative of God's people from Abraham, through the exodus, into the Promised Land, and back from exile. We see in 1 Chronicles 16:8–22, 34–36 that David had used part of Psalms 105 and 106 when he brought the ark into Jerusalem. Later portions of these two psalms, as well as Psalm 107, may have been added after the return from exile in Babylon.

Psalm 105 especially recalls the wandering of the patriarchs in Genesis and the events of the exodus from Egypt, the central narrative of the life and identity of God's Old Testament people. This foreshadows the central events in the entire scope of history when Jesus fulfills God's promises by leading His people out of the domain of death through the waters of Baptism and into the promised land of the new creation.

VISUALIZE

Give Thanks to the LORD, for He Is Good (Psalm 106)

Like Psalm 105, Psalm 106 recounts the events of the Old Testament that were recorded in the books of Exodus and Numbers. This time, though, the emphasis is much more on confessing the sins of God's people both before and after the settling of the Promised Land. Despite the persistent sins of God's people against Him, God is more persistent in His work to bring His people to repentance and forgiveness of sins. Praise the Lord that our God is persistent in forgiving us in Christ!

Book Five, Mostly Songs of Ascents and Praise (Psalms 107–150)

As with Book Four, Book Five of the Psalms includes a selection of songs for a variety of occasions and from many authors. Though a series of similar psalms of praise dominate the end of the book, Book Five also includes songs of teaching and lament.

Let the Redeemed of the LORD Say So (Psalm 107)

Psalm 107 continues the narrative theme of God's deeds in Israel's history from the previous two psalms but describes God bringing His people back from exile in Babylon. This likely was written as a concluding psalm to the previous two, which at least in part were written during the time of David. The central theme is God's ongoing restoration of His people in the Promised Land. This psalm depicts four situations the Israelites had experienced during their exile: those who wandered in the wilderness, those who were imprisoned, those who were foolish, and those who were caught in storms. Powerless to save themselves, the people had cried out to God to save them, and He had been faithful. King Jehoiachin is a great example of the second group, those who were imprisoned, cried out to God, and were released (2 Kings 25:27–30). The psalmist calls on them to thank the Lord for His faithfulness. This psalm reminds us that though we suffer trouble in this life, God has promised us good things and eternal life through Jesus Christ, our Savior.

CLEAR THE CONFUSION

What did sailors in storms have to do with the exiles of Judah (vv. 23–32)?

The Israelites viewed the sea as a dangerous place, a place of trouble. Think of the storm that nearly sank the ship Jonah was on and how he commanded the sailors to throw him into the sea to stop the raging storm. When they threw him in, the waters instantly turned calm, and God provided a large fish to swallow him and save him from drowning (Jonah 1:7–2:10). The psalmist may have chosen this predicament because the people of Judah and Jerusalem had no idea what troubles would come upon them when they were led off into exile. Entering exile was as scary as beginning a voyage across the unknown sea.

PICTURE OF THE SAVIOR

Christ Stills a Storm on the Sea of Galilee

In Mark 4:35–41, Jesus directed His disciples to get into a boat and cross to the other side of the Sea of Galilee. During their voyage, a great windstorm arose and waves broke into the boat. The disciples, several of whom were fishermen well acquainted with this lake from their childhood, were at their wits' end, but Jesus was asleep in the stern of the boat. When they woke Him and asked if He didn't care that they were perishing, Jesus commanded the wind, "Peace!" and the sea, "Be still!" And immediately the wind ceased and a great calm came over the water.

The disciples could very well have sung Psalm 107:23–32 to give their thanks to their Lord and Savior, Jesus Christ.

With God We Shall Do Valiantly (Psalm 108)

This psalm is almost entirely compiled from portions of Psalms 57 and 60. There is no explicit reason given for this novelty, though it may have been compiled postexile from Babylon to emphasize God's help in times of trial.

Help Me, O LORD My God (Psalm 109)

This psalm of David was obviously written at a time when he was attacked by his enemies. This is an imprecatory, or cursing, psalm, and in it he calls for God's curses and judgment to come against his enemies. Today Christians can rightly see our enemies as the fallen powers of the devil, the world, and our sinful flesh. Like David, we can boldly call for God to remove their power so that we and all His creation can be freed from our burdens and serve the Lord unhindered.

CLEAR THE CONFUSION

How could David ask God to do such horrible things to the children of his enemies as he prayed in verses 10–13?

These are difficult passages when Jesus' words "Love your enemies and pray for those who persecute you" (Matthew 5:44) ring in our ears. But first, let us look at the sin of David's enemies. After he had treated them with love, care, and respect and opened his heart to them in friendship (vv. 4–5), they betrayed him, repaying his love and kindness with cursing and pursuing him to cause his death. We might think of Ahithophel, David's trusted counselor, who betrayed him and conspired with David's son Absalom to kill David and seize his throne (2 Samuel 15:12, 30–34; 16:20–23; 17:1–4).

Humanly speaking, it is easy to understand why David would respond with such vehemence against Ahithophel and his descendants. But is that worthy of God's Word that it would be included the Psalms? Should this be our prayer?

Jesus commands us to love our enemies and pray for those who persecute us. He desires to save all sinners, and we should pray the same. But we have spiritual enemies that are beyond repentance and will always be against God—Satan, the sinful world, and our own sinful natures. These will always be opposed to God and seek to destroy us. It is right for us to pray for God to defeat Satan and destroy his works. It is right for us to pray for God to subdue the sinful world, which wars against the church and all that is good and right. And it is right to pray against our sinful nature, which is always against us and will only be stopped when Christ removes it from us when we die or when He returns to judge the living and the dead.

When it comes to sinful people who hurt us, it is right for us to pray for God to empower us to love them and share with them Law and Gospel, through which He can convict them of their sins and draw them to their Savior, Jesus Christ. At the same time, without judging our enemies, we know that those who remain unrepentant fall under God's wrath, and their children will do the same if they follow in their parents' footsteps without ever repenting. So we can ask God to turn all our human enemies to repentance and faith and to do whatever is necessary to stop those who refuse to repent, for the benefit of the church and all believers.

Sit at My Right Hand (Psalm 110)

WAYPOINT

Identify verses in this psalm that tie directly to the person or work of Christ.

How does viewing this and other related psalms as prophecy change your perception of the role of the Psalms?

What does this text show us?

Though short, Psalm 110 is the most quoted in the New Testament of all the psalms—seventeen times! Upon closer inspection, this psalm is an obvious prophecy, of David, of the person and role of the Messiah. Through the power of the Holy Spirit, David saw not only the fulfillment of God's Old Testament prophets but also the person and work of Christ. David's descendant, this mighty warrior priest, would bring about total victory over God's enemies and usher in His peace to His people.

What does this text reveal about God's plan of salvation?

This psalm is richly filled with valuable insight into God's plan of salvation. Verse 1 indicates that David had a Lord who was from God the Father Himself. Jesus indicates in His ministry that He is that Lord (Mark 12:36) who would trample the enemies of God's people. This Lord, Jesus, would rule with the mighty scepter promised to Judah (Genesis 49:10) and serve as a special kind of priest and mediator in the ways of Melchizedek (Genesis 14:18–20). This Melchizedek reference from the psalm would later be discussed in great detail in the book of Hebrews. After prophesying the defeat of God's enemies, the psalm ends with the Lord Messiah drinking from a brook and lifting His head, which has traditionally been interpreted to show Jesus' resurrection after defeating the ancient enemies on the cross.

What does this text uncover about our identity and calling as God's people today?

This incredible short psalm tells us so much about God's great plan of salvation in Christ. It is so easy for us, in our daily routines, to miss the epic nature of what God has done and continues to do for His people in Christ. In reading and meditating on psalms like this one, we can catch an amazing snapshot of the glorious victory of Christ over death and hell, and we can find great comfort in remembering and praising God for what He has done for us.

As you continually read through the Psalms, how will you remind yourself to keep an eye out for prophecies about Jesus?

Great Are the LORD's Works (Psalm 111)

This simple yet powerful psalm of praise serves as a model for Christians today of how to thank God and remember His works. Because He is faithful and remembers His promises, we can fear the Lord and praise His name forever.

The Righteous Will Never Be Moved (Psalm 112)

Psalm 112 continues the theme of praise in this section of the book. Paul quotes verse 9 in 2 Corinthians 9:9 in relationship to how God's people are to steward their resources. Like the psalmist and Paul, we can trust in God in all things and not live in fear of what uncertainties the future may bring.

Who Is like the LORD Our God? (Psalm 113)

Psalm 113 begins a series of psalms that contain six praises sung during the Passover celebration by God's people each year. This psalm and Psalm 114 would have been sung at the very beginning of the Passover celebration. Psalm 113 continues the theme we see throughout the Scriptures of how God brings down the haughty and raises the lowly in His great plan of salvation.

How does knowing that these psalms were sung during the Passover influence your understanding of the worship life of God's Old Testament people?

CLEAR THE CONFUSION

What is the Egyptian Hallel?

Psalms 113–118 as a set are commonly called the Egyptian Hallel. This name is given because these are liturgical psalms used as part of the Passover remembrance by God's people, being an alleluia (Hallel) for God's deliverance from Egypt. Psalms 113–114 would be sung by God's people in their homes before the Passover meal and Psalms 115–118 after. Because of the arrangement and content of these psalms, it is likely that the series would not have been completed until after the return from the Babylonian exile. Jesus and the disciples would have most certainly used these psalms in the Last Supper, culminating in Psalm 118, which includes direct prophecy about the Messiah.

Tremble at the Presence of the Lord (Psalm 114)

This psalm was used, alongside Psalm 113, by God's people at the beginning of each year's Passover meal celebration. Whereas Psalm 113 instructs God's people about who He is, Psalm 114 recalls what God had done. God had freed the people from slavery in Egypt, delivered them through the waters of the Red Sea and the Jordan River on dry ground, and given them manna and water during their journey through the wilderness.

To Your Name Give Glory (Psalm 115)

Scholars suggest that while Psalms 113–114 would have been sung by God's people before the Passover meal, Psalms 115–118 would have been used after the meal was completed. The language in Psalm 115 suggests that it was possibly written and included in the Passover psalms after the return from exile in Babylon. In the psalm, people are instructed to look to God and not the false idols of the pagan nations.

PICTURE OF THE SAVIOR

More Real Than Idols

For Israel, one consequence of living in a land surrounded by hostile, pagan nations was the common exposure to idol worship for many of her citizens. Idols were carved or otherwise-shaped images of false gods that people of other nations would bring with them as they traveled through the land. Contact with these tokens of worship often drew God's people away from

Him by offering a corporeal subject onto which they could heap praise and by which they could have an outward display of strength.

To tackle these concerns, the psalmist took great issue with idols for their many deficiencies when compared to the real and efficacious might of the true God. Unlike idols, our God does not exist through mere lumps of silver and gold but through His Word, which is alive, active, and became flesh as Jesus Christ. Walking on earth as full man and God, Jesus displayed power through signs and miracles, the greatest of which showed His preeminence over even the grave and death itself. Unlike any idol of precious metal from the Old Testament or modern idols of wealth, power, and the self, God powerfully lives and reigns over His entire creation for the sake of His people.

I Love the LORD (Psalm 116)

This fourth of the Passover psalms thanks the Lord for His deliverance of His people from destruction during the exodus. Even more than that, it has been clearly interpreted as a prophecy of Christ—the Messiah praising God for delivering Him from the exodus of death on the cross to the promised land of the resurrection. Christians have used this psalm in their worship services, especially as an offering hymn.

Where do you see the prophecies of Christ in Psalm 116?

CLEAR THE CONFUSION

Why did the psalmist say, "Precious in the sight of the LORD is the death of His saints" (v. 15)?

By all physical appearances, death is defeat. It can also give the impression that God is not strong enough or doesn't care enough to save His servant from death. But this passage shows that God is with us all through our lives, no less as we draw our last breath than when we drew our first breath. It reassures us that as we approach our final moment on earth, our God will be with us, watching closely, ready to carry us to His side.

The LORD's Faithfulness Endures Forever (Psalm 117)

This fifth of the Passover psalms is also the shortest psalm in the Bible. The emphasis of this psalm is, surprisingly, the call for all nations and peoples to praise God! Though the Israelites were God's chosen people, God's desire was and still is that all would hear His Word and be brought to repentance and saving faith.

His Steadfast Love Endures Forever (Psalm 118)

How do the words or phrases of this psalm reveal who God is and what He has done for us?

In what ways do you see prophecies of Christ in this psalm?

How can you focus on Christ as your King today?

As you read through Psalm 119, ask yourself how this entire psalm paints a grand picture of how Christians should approach God's Word in our daily lives.

WAYPOINT

What does this text show us?
As the final of the Passover psalms, this would have been sung by God's people at the culmination of the Passover ceremony. The context hints that it might have originally been written as a celebration psalm of David or at the dedication of the second temple after the return from exile. Regardless, the words and phrases of this psalm celebrate national deliverance. It had such a place in the minds of God's people that the crowds chanted verse 26 when Jesus entered Jerusalem on Palm Sunday (John 12:13). In the psalm, we see a call for salvation and a prayer that God will save.

What does this text reveal about God's plan of salvation?
Though originally used by the Israelites at the Passover meal as a song of national deliverance, this psalm is clearly also a prophecy of Christ. He is the stone the builders rejected who has become the cornerstone (v. 22). On Palm Sunday, the people waved palm branches (a symbol of the Jewish people) and cried out the essence of this psalm. Though Jesus was not the kind of king many of them expected, His deliverance would be greater than any of them could have imagined or hoped for. Instead of delivering the Jews from the Roman Empire, Jesus delivered all peoples from the ultimate powers of sin, death, and the devil.

What does this text uncover about our identity and calling as God's people today?
It is easy to fall into the trap of looking to current-day political figures for salvation. Yes, as part of our vocation as a citizen of our country, we should care about what is going on in society and act upon what is good and right. Politicians and policies, however, are temporary. Our ultimate allegiance is to the King of kings, the Christ who came into Jerusalem that first Palm Sunday to overcome the power of death for us. As we live our lives in our world today, let us keep our eyes fixed on Christ above all earthly or human powers. Let us also look to the day when He comes again on the clouds of glory to make all things new and to establish His eternal kingdom in the new heavens and the new earth.

Your Word Is a Lamp to My Feet (Psalm 119)

The date and occasion of this psalm are uncertain. Portions resemble Psalm 19, which would suggest an earlier date in the kingdom of God's people. Other commentators suggest either a fifth- or sixth-century BC date, around the time of the exile or return from captivity. The author identifies himself as a young man (vv. 9, 99, 100) who is lying in bonds (v. 61) and awaiting death (v. 109). The writers of the Lutheran Confessions attribute this to David (Solid Declaration of the Formula of Concord, Article II, paragraph 15). Regardless of the actual author, the psalmist is concerned primarily with meditating on God's Word and instructing others to do so.

CLEAR THE CONFUSION

What's going on in Psalm 119?

Psalm 119 is the longest of the psalms—and the longest chapter in the Bible. It is also a complex and often misunderstood psalm. It is an acrostic poem; that is, it works through the twenty-two letters of the Hebrew alphabet. It is divided into twenty-two sections of eight verses each; each section corresponds with a letter (with one exception) of the Hebrew alphabet, and each verse begins with that letter. Though some commentators have stated that there is little to no organization to this psalm, others have disagreed.

One way to view the progression of thought from the author is this: the psalmist moves from a concern for God's Law (Aleph to He) to his own distress (Waw to Kaph) then back to God's Law (Lamedh to Nun) then to distress at the wickedness of God's enemies (Samekh to Tsadhe) and finally to a closing pledge of obedience (Qoph to Taw).

It should also be noted that the author uses the word *law* frequently, but this should not be understood as the way Paul later uses the word *law*—that word that points out and convicts us of sin. Instead, the word *law* in Psalm 119 is meant to be understood interchangeably with other words such as *testimonies*, *precepts*, *commandments*, and *promises*. These are different ways of referring to God's Word—both Law and Gospel—which in this psalm mostly is used to refer to God's communication to us that will guide us to walk in His ways through life.

ALEPH (119:1–8)

The psalmist begins not only by praising God for His righteous Word but also by pledging with God's help to be faithful to God's statutes and to keep his eyes on God's commandments. He models an attitude of great reverence for and understanding of how God's Word gives guidance to life.

Beth (119:9–16)

He continues by describing how meditating on, storing up (memorizing), and speaking God's Word is the highest virtue any young man can have. This is no less true today, as God's Word not only gives instruction on avoiding sin but also grants eternal life to those who believe it.

Gimel (119:17–24)

Given that God's Word is to be treasured, the psalmist then prays for God's help in keeping his eyes focused on that Word. He expresses sorrow over the scoffers and persecutors who constantly mock him for his adherence to God's Word. This prayer is worth emulating in our lives today.

Daleth (119:25–32)

The psalmist also prays for strength to keep and meditate on God's Word, as his sinful flesh is weak. Christians today continue this prayer, as we boldly ask the Spirit to open our hearts and minds and teach us to delight in living God's way as we, too, meditate on the Scriptures.

He (119:33–40)

Surrounded by so many worthless distractions and worldly temptations, the psalmist also prays for God's preservation in the paths of righteousness. In a world that constantly assaults us with all sorts of sinful diversions, we are wise to follow the lead of the psalmist's prayer for steadfast concentration on God's Word.

?

How does the psalmist's distress in this psalm mirror our own as we strive to live faithfully in this broken world?

Waw (119:41–48)

The psalmist then turns the direction of the psalm for a time toward his own distress. He prays that he would be able to give a worthy confession of his faith before those who oppose him. With this God-given guidance by His Word, the psalmist will be emboldened to speak God's truth joyfully even to kings.

Zayin (119:49–56)

In the midst of his affliction, the psalmist prays that God would remember His promises to His people. The psalmist also speaks of his zeal for God's Word in the face of wicked opposition. May Christians today have a similar passion for meditating on and keeping God's commandments!

Heth (119:57–64)

Though surrounded by wickedness, the psalmist remembers and cleaves to God's Word. He also clings to fellow believers in his trials. Christians are not meant to live solitary lives of faith; we are meant to live in the community of God's people, receiving His gifts together and building one another up in all circumstances.

Teth (119:65–72)

The psalmist then recalls a peaceful time when he wandered from God's Word and was afflicted. This suffering brought the psalmist back to God's Word and God's truth, for which the psalmist thanks God. Though Christians do not have to call bad times good, we can thank God for using humbling circumstances to teach us to repent and to trust in His Word above all things, like the psalmist.

Yodh (119:73–80)

Even so, the psalmist still acknowledges his continual need for God's aid. He prays earnestly for comfort in his suffering and justice against those who have falsely accused him. Though we rejoice in the mercy we've been given in Christ, we, too, can still pray earnestly for God's aid in our present trials.

Kaph (119:81–88)

Concluding this section of the psalm that deals with the psalmist's distress, he cries out a prayer for help. The affliction given by his enemies has taken its toll, and in essence, he cries out, "How long?" Christians today are likewise surrounded by the fallen powers of the devil, the world, and our sinful flesh, and we, too, are bold to cry out, "Come, Lord Jesus!"

Lamedh (119:89–96)

The psalm then turns back to more direct reflection on the power of God's Word. The author praises God for His eternal, unchanging Word, praising God for His salvation by it. We, too, can praise the Word of God, who took on flesh to die on the cross and rise again for our eternal salvation.

What can we learn from the psalmist's example about what our attitude should be toward God's Word?

Mem (119:97–104)

The psalmist continues by extolling how God's Word makes him wiser than his enemies, his teachers, and the aged. These eternal teachings of God direct his way and keep him from evil. In such days as these, Christians, too, should meditate on God's Word, which brings about wisdom and understanding of God's ways.

Nun (119:105–112)

The psalmist uses a powerful and well-known illustration for God's Word: a light to his feet. Though enemies lay snares and traps on the sides of the way of righteousness, those who keep God's Word as a lamp to guide their way will not fall into those snares. Though surrounded and afflicted by the fallen powers, we, too, find direction and truth in God's Word as we navigate through life.

Samekh (119:113–120)

The psalmist then turns away from the theme of direct reflection on God's Word and to his distress over the wickedness of God's enemies. He despises those who oppose the truth of God's Word and calls upon God to be a shield and protection for him. Though we are called to love our neighbor, even those who hate us, we, too, can zealously despise the fallen powers of the devil, the world, and our sinful nature.

Ayin (119:121–128)

Though facing oppression and opposition, the psalmist confesses his faith that God will not abandon him. The psalmist continues to cling not only to God's Word but also to God's steadfast love and promises. Even in the hardest days, Christians can likewise cling to God's unchanging Word and promises.

Pe (119:129–136)

The psalmist continues by once again focusing on calling for help from the Lord. His eyes stream tears of sorrow for those who do not keep God's commandments. Nevertheless, the psalmist counts on God's promises and relies on God's mercy to redeem him from oppression.

Tsadhe (119:137–144)

The final verses of this section in which the psalmist cries out in distress focus on his humility. He is small (young) and in anguish, but God is great and righteous and true. What a wonderful reminder for God's people today to recall our humility and rejoice in God's faithfulness and grace.

Qoph (119:145–152)

The final four portions of Psalm 119 constitute a pledge of obedience to God's Word. Here, the psalmist declares that he calls out day and night to God, placing his hope in God's Word. Christians can follow this example by establishing periodic set times of prayer and meditation on God's Word in our daily routines, both on our own and with our household.

How can you follow the psalmist's example in pledging to abide in God's Word in your daily life?

Resh (119:153–160)

The pledge of obedience to God's Word continues with the psalmist's earnest acknowledgment that God's Word revives and gives life. Though adversaries, including the devil, the world, and the sinful flesh, surround the psalmist, God's Word will not fail to grant him faith and life.

Sin and Shin (119:161–168)

Though falsely accused and persecuted by princes, the psalmist will stand in awe of God's Word. He proclaims that God gives peace, even in the midst of opposition, to those who love God and His Word. In a world so desperately seeking peace, Christians can likewise proclaim God's truth, which brings life and salvation.

Taw (119:169–176)

The psalm concludes with a final pledge of faithfulness to God's Word, as well as with prayers for understanding. The final verse is revealing when seen within God's epic plan of salvation. The psalmist cries that he has gone astray like a sheep but calls on God's love and mercy to rescue him. Jesus is the Good Shepherd (John 10:11–15), who seeks the lost sheep (Luke 15:3–5). The prayer of deliverance of the psalmist, and the prayers of God's people for all time for salvation, are fulfilled in Jesus.

SET THE SCENE

Pilgrimages

Psalms 120–134 all have a similar superscription: "A Song of Ascents." Though unclear as to the exact meaning of this label, it's likely that they were to be sung at the temple courts and/or by Israelites on pilgrimages to Jerusalem for festivals. Because of its elevation, Jerusalem was always a place to which one "ascended" to while on a journey. The Torah commanded that three times a year the males should appear before the tabernacle for a feast (Exodus 34:23). In Deuteronomy, God adds further that these feasts would be the Feast of

Unleavened Bread (Passover), the Feast of Weeks, and the Feast of Booths (Deuteronomy 16:16). For these times, God's people would make journeys to the tabernacle (and then later to the temple) with their households for the holy days, and it is likely that these songs of ascents were sung collectively by the pilgrims on their way to celebrate. The Scriptures record Jesus Himself as a child making His way to the Feast of the Passover in Jerusalem with His family (Luke 2:41–43). It is likely that Jesus would have sung these psalms on the road each time His family made these pilgrimages. It was also during one of these pilgrimages, while so many of God's people were gathered together in Jerusalem for the Feast of Weeks (Pentecost), that the Holy Spirit was first poured out in a special way upon the church. The songs of ascents were likely also sung by these pilgrims as they traveled from around the world to celebrate together.

Deliver Me, O LORD (Psalm 120)

Based on context clues, this first song of ascents was likely composed after the return from the Babylonian exile. In the psalm, the anonymous psalmist pleads to God in distress over enemies who surround him. Their tongues, like weapons, spread deceit and stir conflict. Despite the false accusations of enemies, God always speaks truth and offers peace through Christ.

My Help Comes from the LORD (Psalm 121)

What words or phrases stick out to you as you consider Psalm 121? Why?

This song of ascents has been a comfort to many throughout the centuries. It is a reminder that God is with us throughout our earthly pilgrimage. We do well to focus on Him when anything in creation brings us fear. He has promised never to abandon us, and ultimately He will keep us forever in the new creation.

Let Us Go to the House of the LORD (Psalm 122)

This song of ascents was obviously written during or after the reign of David, when he captured Jerusalem and made it his capital city. In it, the psalmist marvels at and prays for the city in which the Israelites gathered for their annual festivals. Christians today look to the new Jerusalem that descends from heaven in the new creation as we journey through this life.

Our Eyes Look to the LORD Our God (Psalm 123)

This song of ascents does not include travel imagery. Instead, it directs our eyes heavenward, where God sits on His throne above all who hold His people in contempt. Surrounded by scorners and the proud in this life, in our weariness, we, too, keep our eyes directed at our King of kings sitting on the throne of heaven, and we wait patiently for Him to judge the proud mockers.

Our Help Is in the Name of the LORD (Psalm 124)

This is one of three songs of ascents ascribed to David. The context may point either to a time when Saul was pursuing David or to a reflection upon God leading His people through the exodus. Regardless, whether we face overpowering peril or hidden, subtle plots of our enemies, especially Satan, we rejoice. Line 1 of the final verse—"Our help is in the name of the Lord"—is a wonderful comfort to God's people for all time.

?

How does the idea that the songs of ascents were part of the pilgrimage songs of God's people impact how you read them? Why?

The LORD Surrounds His People (Psalm 125)

The context clues of this psalm of ascents suggest it was written during the postexilic time of Nehemiah. The author uses the image of the hills surrounding Jerusalem (the hill of Zion is in a kind of valley) as an illustration for God's care and protection of His people as He guards them from all wickedness.

Restore Our Fortunes, O LORD (Psalm 126)

Like the previous psalm, this song of ascents was likely composed after the return from exile in Babylon. The author, and those who sing this song, rejoice in God's favor. Their restoration to Jerusalem from captivity was like waking up, thinking that they had only dreamed that things had turned for the better but that they were still in desperate straits, only to learn that it was all true—they really were free. For Christians today, we look forward to the day when Jesus will wake us from the sleep of death to rise to newness of life in the restored creation.

Unless the LORD Builds the House (Psalm 127)

This one song of ascents attributed to Solomon reads like a proverb. It extols the virtue and value of having children. Yet unless those who raise children raise them in the love of God and His Word, that labor is in vain. What an important reminder for God's people for all time to raise up the next generation to fear, love, and trust in God above all things.

Blessed Is Everyone Who Fears the LORD (Psalm 128)

What does it mean to properly fear the Lord? According to these psalms, why is it so important?

Psalm 128 is similar to the previous song of ascents in holding up the value of the family. It counts the relationships between husband and wife and between parents and the children God has given us as true blessings from God. May we, too, properly fear the Lord and walk in His ways all our days, turning to Him for forgiveness, mercy, and grace through Christ.

They Have Afflicted Me from My Youth (Psalm 129)

The context of Psalm 129 suggests that it was written after the return from Babylonian exile. The psalmist cries out to God concerning his affliction, likening it to being put under a plow. Yet Christians know that ultimately our afflictions will finally be removed by Christ in the new creation, because He has conquered the fallen powers for us on the cross.

CLEAR THE CONFUSION

What are "the cords of the wicked" (v. 4) that God has cut?

They are the cords that connect the harness of the oxen to the plows of the wicked who were scourging Israel in verse 3. In other words, God has stopped the oppressors from oppressing Israel.

My Soul Waits for the Lord (Psalm 130)

What words or phrases from Psalm 130 can help you better understand the role of confession and repentance in your life?

This is not only a song of ascents but also one of the penitential psalms. In Psalm 130, we see the anguish of one crying for forgiveness turned into joy by remembering the redeeming promise of God! This psalm exemplifies the power of God's Law, which shows us our sin and brings about repentance, and the Gospel, which reveals our Savior, Jesus Christ, who grants us redemption and forgiveness. Note especially how verse 8 points ahead to Jesus, the Son of God, who will redeem us from all our sins.

I Have Calmed and Quieted My Soul (Psalm 131)

The contextual clues suggest David may have written this psalm as an expression of his humility (see 2 Samuel 6:20–22). It is easy in life to get overwhelmed with matters beyond our control, especially when we begin to wonder why and how God works like He does. This psalm reminds us to slow down and keep the perspective that God's ways are not our ways. Instead of feeling out of control, we can put our hope and trust in the Lord.

LINK BETWEEN THE TESTAMENTS

I Have Calmed and Quieted My Soul → The Faith of a Child (Psalm 131:1–3 → Matthew 18:1–6)

To children, everything in the world seems gargantuan. That is the perspective David hoped to capture in this short psalm, which focuses on the calm and quiet found in simply approaching God and resting in His presence. Comparing himself to a weaned child, David urges his audience to yearn for that rest as well, for there one finds the trusting, simple, and earnest faith of a child toward his parents.

Christ would later lift up an example of faith using the disposition of children: "Truly, I say to you, unless you turn and become like children, you will never enter the kingdom of heaven. Whoever humbles himself like this child is the greatest in the kingdom of heaven" (Matthew 18:3–4). Indeed, Christ came not as an awe-inspiring man but as a little child laid in a manger, and He lifted up children as the primary inheritors of the kingdom of heaven. Sometimes, it's good to simply approach God and be at peace in the joy that has come through Christ's awesome work for you and me.

The LORD Has Chosen Zion (Psalm 132)

This song of ascents has no author attributed to it, but as it remembers and celebrates David's bringing the ark of the covenant into Jerusalem, it was likely written around the time of Solomon for the dedication of the temple. It underscores God's promise to David that one of his descendants would sit on his throne forever (see 2 Samuel 7). The Son of David, Jesus, ultimately fulfilled and still fulfills this promise.

CLEAR THE CONFUSION

What does "His footstool" (v. 7) refer to?

God sits on His throne in heaven but is specially present above the cherubim on the cover of the ark. So the ark of the covenant is known as God's footstool, His dwelling place on earth.

After reading the songs of ascents, what most struck you about the series?

LINK BETWEEN THE TESTAMENTS

The Lord Has Chosen Zion → The Great Multitude (Psalm 132 → Revelation 7:9–17)

Not only does this song of ascents bring its audience back to when the ark and the temple were united, but its words also prepare the reader for the larger gathering of God's people as His church grows and ultimately for the great jubilee of the multitude John describes in the book of Revelation. A portion of the psalm's call to celebration beseeches God, saying, "Arise, O LORD, and go to Your resting place, You and the ark of Your might. Let Your priests be clothed with righteousness, and let Your saints shout for joy" (vv. 8–9). Having been completed when the ark was moved to its rightful place, the temple represented the place where God descended to be among His people, for under normal circumstances, His holiness would make such a meeting impossible.

Thankfully, there is no separation between God and His people in heaven, as John reports, preparing us with his witness of all the saints shouting praise to God on His throne:

> After this I looked, and behold, a great multitude that no one could number, from every nation, from all tribes and peoples and languages, standing before the throne and before the Lamb, clothed in white robes, with palm branches in their hands, and crying out with a loud voice, "Salvation belongs to our God who sits on the throne, and to the Lamb!" (Revelation 7:9–10)

Thanks be to Christ, who has made it possible for such a glorious sight by His precious blood!

When Brothers Dwell in Unity (Psalm 133)

This song of ascents, attributed to David, uses a powerful and unusual image to celebrate the unity of God's people: the ceremony in which Aaron was ordained as Israel's first high priest. Then it adds the refreshing dew that falls on dry, parched land. The church today can also celebrate our unity as God's people when we gather around our great High Priest, Jesus Christ, as He gives us His gifts in the Divine Service.

SET THE SCENE

Anointing Oil

In the Old Testament, pressed oil from olives had many uses. It was often used medicinally or therapeutically to help soothe skin, like the lotions we use today. A good host would offer oil to a weary visitor as an act of hospitality. It was also poured over the heads of the priests to anoint them for their special priestly service (see Exodus 30:22–33). In Psalm 133, the mental picture of oil pouring down the beard of the priest would have evoked not only the image of God's care through the priests but also the blessed unity of God's people gathered together in His healing peace.

Come, Bless the LORD (Psalm 134)

This is both the last and shortest of the songs of ascents, a series which started with Psalm 120. The psalmist urges the priests, who were on duty at the temple day and night, to bless the Lord. Then, the psalmist prays that God would bless them in return. As we praise God our Creator in worship, we know that we, too, are blessed through Christ.

Your Name, O LORD, Endures Forever (Psalm 135)

The context indicates that this psalm was meant to be sung in the temple by the whole gathering of God's people. It recalls important historical events in God's plan of salvation up to that point. Through the words of the psalm, God's people also condemn the foolish practice of idol worship and focus on united worship of the true God.

His Steadfast Love Endures Forever (Psalm 136)

Psalm 136 is unique in that the entire song is divided into a call-and-response refrain. It is likely that it was used as a group liturgy, with the leader singing one line and the congregation responding, "For His steadfast love endures forever." What a wonderful model for Christians today to have on our hearts and lips the glorious praise that God's steadfast love endures forever for us in Christ and is the reason for everything He has done, does today, and will do for us forever.

Imagine you were in the courts of the Old Testament temple when Psalm 136 was being chanted. Based on the words, what do you think the experience would have been like? What would the attitude of the worshipers have been?

How Shall We Sing the LORD's Song? (Psalm 137)

This difficult imprecatory (cursing) psalm recalls the experience of God's people in exile, calling upon God to pour out His wrath on those who had oppressed them. Today we live in a form of exile in the world. We await the day when the world will be finally overcome and death will be undone at the resurrection. Until then, we pray that God would hinder and destroy the plans of the fallen powers that seek to destroy the church.

CLEAR THE CONFUSION

Psalm 137 is disturbing, so why is it in the Bible?

Few passages in the Scriptures are more troubling than some of those found in Psalm 137, especially verse 9. The psalmist calls those who murder the children of the Babylonians blessed. What's going on here? God had called on His people in the Old Testament to remain faithful to Him, yet they repeatedly turned to false gods and rejected the Lord. Eventually, God brought His righteous wrath upon them first through the Assyrians and then through the Babylonians, who not only invaded but also delighted in massacring untold thousands of men, women, and children in their conquests. God confronted their savage cruelty in Isaiah 47:5–6. God's people had seen with their own eyes the brutal and horrifying consequences of their sins and had experienced firsthand God's wrath and judgment in their households at the hands of the invaders. But the Assyrians and Babylonians had reacted with savage and gleeful cruelty.

Psalm 137 recalls the sorrow of God's people in exile in Babylon, conquered and displaced, with the Babylonians mocking them and their God. The people of Judah, battered and beaten down, remember and appreciate what they themselves had foolishly given up. In a scathing prayer, they ask that God would bring upon the unrepentant Babylonians the same wrath for their sin that they had endured because of theirs.

The reality is that a final judgment awaits all people for all time at the end of this world. The brutal judgment enacted in Psalm 137 will be nothing compared to the unending torment in hell that will strike all unrepentant evildoers at the world's end. Yet those who are brought to repentance and faith in Christ will be saved. God wants us to proclaim Christ to the world so that more may hear, be brought to faith, and escape that horrendous punishment. At the same time, we can call out for God's judgment against

?

How can the cursing, or imprecatory, psalms help us bring to God the hurt, anger, and suffering that result when other people sin against us? How does the suffering of Jesus on the cross help us move beyond cursing to praying for the people who hurt us?

His enemies, looking to the day when His wrath will be poured out on Satan and all the fallen powers of hell that oppose God and seek to tear down His righteous reign on earth.

Give Thanks to the LORD (Psalm 138)

Psalm 138 is attributed to David, though the reference to the temple may mean it was either dedicated to David or perhaps written by David in the anticipation of his son Solomon building the temple in Jerusalem. The psalm's depiction of the king's victory over his enemies and relationship to God prefigures Christ, the final true King of kings, who wins the victory over sin, death, and hell for us.

Search Me, O God, and Know My Heart (Psalm 139)

WAYPOINT

What does this text show us?

This famous psalm of David takes the reader on a journey. It begins with acknowledging the truth that God knows us better than we know ourselves. There is no place we can escape God's presence: heaven, in death, the horizon, the sea, the darkness, or the light. Yet even in His greatness, God still cares for us. God formed us in our conception. The journey ends with a call for God to judge those who oppose Him. Seeing all that God has revealed to David about who David is and how God loves him, David expresses zeal for following God's ways.

What does this text reveal about God's plan of salvation?

Psalm 139 is a study in contrasts. On one hand, we see an unsearchable God who knows all things and is everywhere. On the other hand, we see a God who cares deeply about each one of His human creatures, forming them and preparing them for the days ahead. Throughout the Scriptures, we see this tension: God is so much greater than us that we can never understand Him, yet God intimately cares for us better than we care for ourselves. This tension is ultimately seen in Christ. The God of the universe chooses to put on human flesh and dwell among us. He willingly goes to the cross to redeem us from our sins and rises to new life to overcome death for us. The God who knows all things willingly chooses to suffer and die for us so that we can be with Him forever.

?

If you were to make a movie depicting Psalm 139, what would you choose to include? How would you go about directing it?

?

What does this psalm reveal to you about the nature of God's love for you?

How can you work to better value all life in your congregation? your family? your neighborhood?

What does this text uncover about our identity and calling as God's people today?

Psalm 139 is often used as a text to show what God thinks about human life. It is precious to Him, even from the time of conception. We live in a sin-sick and broken world with many different thoughts about the value of life. Though each person is unique, and many will experience physical or mental difficulties, the reality remains that all life from conception is valuable to God. As such, Christians should also value life from the womb to the tomb and seek to care for our neighbor in all circumstances, just as Christ cares for us.

Deliver Me, O LORD, from Evil Men (Psalm 140)

This psalm of David is one of the cursing, or imprecatory, psalms. During his life, David was constantly pursued by the plots and accusations of evil men who opposed God. Though the calls for judgment against them may sound harsh and unloving to our ears, they reveal a deeper reality in God's plan of salvation. Those who afflict the poor, the weak, and the oppressed and those who oppose His anointed (especially Christ) and refuse to repent will receive God's wrath at the final judgment.

CLEAR THE CONFUSION

What did David mean when he said, "You have covered my head in the day of battle" (v. 7)?

Like a helmet, God had protected him from the deadly blows of his enemies.

Give Ear to My Voice (Psalm 141)

The occasion of this psalm may have been when David was driven out of Jerusalem by his treasonous son Absalom and could not worship on Mount Zion. Exiled from his place of worship and pursued by those who hated him, all David could do is offer up his prayers instead of incense, which was used in worship. Likewise, the prayers of God's people today are not insignificant. God desires that we bring these before Him and trust that He hears them.

You Are My Refuge (Psalm 142)

The Scriptures record two instances when David hid from Saul in a cave (see 1 Samuel 22; 24). While in this situation, as expressed in Psalm 142, David cries out to God as one imprisoned and trapped on all sides.

Yet we know that God answered David's prayer and delivered him, just as we know He has delivered us from the prison of our sin by David's descendant Jesus.

PICTURE OF THE SAVIOR

Persecuted, Tortured, Deserted Savior

David's desperate prayer allows us to sneak a peek at the kind of life Jesus lived in the face of those who hated Him. Fleeing from King Saul's wrath, David hid in the depths of a cave to avoid his assailant and felt buried in the depths of sin and betrayal. His vivid experience is a physical image of sin's imprisoning effect in our lives, barring us from one another and God. Jesus would suffer a similar, magnified trial in life and unto death; tortured and despised by the ruling authorities, He would be buried in a cave after hanging on the cross. Thankfully, that was not the end of the story. Jesus rose again so that those trapped in the tombs of their own sin might be freed and live eternally through faith in Him.

My Soul Thirsts for You (Psalm 143)

In this last of the penitential, or repentance, psalms, David cries out for God's mercy. This may have been written on the occasion of David's exile after the rebellion of his son Absalom. Regardless, God's people can learn from David's example to boldly and humbly come before God's throne in repentance, knowing that He hears our prayers and desires to forgive our sins.

My Rock and My Fortress (Psalm 144)

Using military imagery, David sings for joy at victory over his enemies. We are all naturally born as sinful enemies of God, but through the means of grace (the Scriptures and the Sacraments) God brings us into His family and makes us His children. With David, and with all who have gone before, we, too, can praise Him for being our victory and our refuge.

Great Is the LORD (Psalm 145)

This song of David is the only with the superscription "A Song of Praise," which is literally translated "a psalm." It is often referred to as "the mission psalm," as it extols God's people from generation to generation to share God's Word not only with others in the community of God's people but also to all "the children of man" (v. 12). Our King, Jesus

What does Psalm 145 show you about how God's people should approach mission work?

Christ, desires that none should perish but that all hear, come to faith, and join in His glorious kingdom, which has no end.

Put Not Your Trust in Princes (Psalm 146)

The last five psalms make up a series often called the "hallelujah psalms," as they each begin with the phrase "Praise the Lord!" Though not evident in the Hebrew superscriptions, the Greek translation of the Old Testament attributed these to the postexilic prophets Haggai and Zechariah. Here, the psalmist directs God's people to trust not in earthly powers or humans but in God, who alone gives eternal salvation.

He Heals the Brokenhearted (Psalm 147)

This second hallelujah psalm memorializes the rebuilding of Jerusalem after the return from Babylonian exile. In it, the psalmist (likely Haggai or Zechariah) praises God for His marvelous works and blessings. We look forward to the day when, at the resurrection, God will gather His people from across time to the new Jerusalem.

Praise the Name of the LORD (Psalm 148)

This third hallelujah psalm surveys all of God's created order, calling on all of creation from the stars to the snowflakes to praise Him. At the end of this list the psalmist places God's people, the lead singers of this choir of praise to their Creator.

CLEAR THE CONFUSION

What does it mean that creation praises God?

Psalm 148 follows the pattern of many of the psalms that indicate creation itself somehow praises God. How can this be? Can a star or a snowflake speak words of praise? Obviously not. Instead, this serves as a powerful metaphor for the state and witness of creation. First, the intricacies of creation, from smallest to largest, confess God's intelligent design behind the universe. Though this corrupted nature cannot in itself fully reveal who God is, it does reveal that there is a God. Second, Paul speaks about how all of this fallen, broken creation is groaning in anticipation of the new creation (Romans 8:19–22). Just as humans will be remade and restored at the resurrection, so, too, will all of creation. Natural disasters and changes are signs that the world is not as it should be and that the natural order needs to be restored. In anticipation of this, Jesus Himself stated that if man should refuse to praise God, the stones themselves would cry out (Luke 19:40). All of creation desperately needs restoration, and only in Christ at the end of all things will it be fully restored.

Sing to the LORD a New Song (Psalm 149)

This fourth hallelujah psalm seems to describe a festival procession to the Temple Mount. Notable in this is the image of salvation being a kind of adornment, something that God gives His people. Because of this gift, God's people can boldly sing praises of God's power and dominion over all things.

Let Everything Praise the LORD (Psalm 150)

This final hallelujah psalm, and the final psalm of the Bible, highlights the role of music in temple worship. In ten lines, the unnamed psalmist lists various instruments used in worship, culminating with the mighty shout of the voices of all of God's people: "Praise the Lord!" (v. 6). May God's people today continually have this shout of praise on our lips!

?

If it's true that the last five psalms were written at the very end of the Old Testament time, what do they show us about life as God's people in those four hundred years of waiting before Christ came?

PROVERBS

Welcome to Proverbs

King Solomon wrote three books of the Bible: the Song of Solomon, Proverbs, and Ecclesiastes. He wrote the Song of Solomon early in his reign, Proverbs in the middle, and Ecclesiastes at the end, after he walked away from God's promises.

The book of Proverbs is a collection of wise sayings written by King Solomon—a man renowned for his great wisdom—and other authors. Some of these sayings were collected in Solomon's time; others were added later to this collection, such as a collection of Solomon's sayings that pertained to kings and kingly courts recorded in the days of faithful King Hezekiah (chapters 25–29).

At first glance, these wise sayings may appear to be a collection of random sayings. But in the original Hebrew, the writings are far from random, and the true character of Proverbs becomes more apparent.

The sequence of proverbs in the book guides the reader in the way of godly wisdom and living. As you read through Proverbs, examine your life and priorities and ask God to give you a heart of wisdom to repent of your sins, to trust in Jesus Christ (who alone makes you righteous in God's sight), and to help you walk the straight and narrow road with your Savior and your fellow Christians.

Which proverbs are already familiar to you?

Proverbs at a Glance

- **Start:** The book of Proverbs begins with a father imparting wisdom to his son.
- **End:** The book of Proverbs concludes with a poem concerning the characteristics of an ideal wife.
- **Theme:** The theme of the book of Proverbs is expressed clearly in 1:7: "The fear of the LORD is the beginning of knowledge; fools despise wisdom and instruction."
- **Author and Date:** The book of Proverbs is one of only two books in the Bible with multiple known authors—the other being the book of Psalms. While the majority of the wise sayings recorded

in Proverbs were written and gathered by King Solomon, there are also contributions from Agur, Lemuel, Lemuel's mother, and an unnamed wise man. The majority of the book was written in the tenth century BC, but some proverbs may have been recorded during the late eighth or early seventh century BC.

- **Places Visited:** The book of Proverbs has no particular locations since there are no narratives contained in the book.
- **Journey Time:** The thirty-one chapters of Proverbs can be read in under two hours.
- **Outline:**
  - Introduction and Discourses on Wisdom (1:1–9:18)
  - The Proverbs of Solomon (10:1–22:16)
  - Proverbs from Wise People (22:17–24:34)
  - Solomon's Proverbs Recorded by Hezekiah (25:1–29:27)
  - Agur's Proverbs (30:1–33)
  - King Lemuel's Proverbs and a Poem About an Ideal Wife (31:1–31)

Five Top Sights and Spectacles of Proverbs

Trust in the Lord (3:1–12) Listen to a father's instruction to his son concerning the benefits of trusting the Lord's wisdom.

Contrasting Wisdom and Folly (9:1–18) Attend a banquet to learn the differences between wisdom and folly.

Don't Be a Fool! (17:7–22:16) Heed Solomon's warnings against living like a fool.

A King's Leadership Guide (27:23–29:27) Learn from Solomon's guidebook for faithful leaders.

A Poem Concerning a Wise Wife (31:10–31) Review this poem concerning the traits of an ideal wife.

Seeing Jesus in Proverbs

The book of Proverbs clearly points to God as the only true source of wisdom. Further, the Scriptures identify the Second Person of the Trinity as that source. In the New Testament, Paul makes this assertion clear: "But to those who are called, both Jews and Greeks, Christ the power of God and the wisdom of God. . . . And because of Him you are in Christ Jesus, who became to us wisdom from God, righteousness and sanctification and redemption" (1 Corinthians 1:24, 30).

Paul is not the only one who identifies Jesus as the true source of wisdom. King Solomon was recognized throughout the Scriptures for his great wisdom, yet Matthew and Luke identify someone greater than Solomon. "The queen of the South will rise up at the judgment with this generation and condemn it, for she came from the ends of the earth to hear the wisdom of Solomon, and behold, something greater than Solomon is here" (Matthew 12:42; see also Luke 11:31).

Jesus further identifies Himself as Wisdom incarnate. In Luke 11:49, He says, "Therefore also the Wisdom of God said, 'I will send them prophets and apostles, some of whom they will kill and persecute.'" In the parallel account in Matthew 23:34, He says, "Therefore I send you prophets and wise men and scribes, some of whom you will kill and crucify, and some you will flog in your synagogues and persecute from town to town".

Introduction and Discourses on Wisdom (1:1–9:18)

After introducing the book and its purpose, Solomon provides lengthy lessons praising the value of wisdom and encouraging all readers to pursue it. His lessons encourage all of us to turn from sin and folly and pursue wisdom and the fear of the Lord.

The Beginning of Knowledge (1:1–7)

Solomon begins his collection of wisdom proverbs by establishing the positive benefits of heeding the words of wisdom. Fools despise the wisdom of God, while those who fear the Lord grow in wisdom and understanding.

CLEAR THE CONFUSION

What does it mean to "fear the LORD"?

Solomon concluded his introduction to the subject of wisdom with the exhortation that "the fear of the LORD is the beginning of knowledge" (1:7). This same exhortation appears in the explanation of the First Commandment in Luther's Small Catechism: "You shall have no other gods. *What does this mean?* We should fear, love, and trust in God above all things."

?

What does it mean to you to fear the Lord? Has your understanding of this special "fear" changed for you over your lifetime? What part does respect and honor play in this kind of fear? What does it mean to fear God's wrath?

But the "fear of the Lord" is not to be equated with being afraid of the Lord. While we should certainly live in terror at the thought of letting our sinful desires turn us from Christ, we need not fear the punishment we rightly deserve because of our sinfulness. Instead, we live under the love of God, shown to us through the death and resurrection of Christ for our sins. We respect and honor Him by trusting in His promise to bring us to be with Him for all eternity. Then we let His Word turn us from our sinful desires and direct our life on earth.

So the fear of the Lord is the beginning of our wise relationship with our God and Father. This fear leads to an understanding of who God is and what He has done for us through His Son and to a great love and respect for Him.

? What kinds of enticements happened in the time of Solomon against which he warns his son here? What kinds of sinful actions does Satan tempt us to pursue through the pressure of those around us today? How can we avoid these temptations that would lead us to abandon God?

The Enticement of Sinners (1:8–19)

A father warns his son against the temptations of sinners. Peers often tempt believers of every age to ignore their father's instruction and their mother's teaching. Sinners call to the righteous, seeking to lead them astray. Sinners seek personal gain and are willing to spill the blood of their victims—that is, take their possessions, harm them, and even kill them.

The Call of Wisdom (1:20–33)

Wisdom is personified as a woman calling aloud to all who will listen. Those who turn and follow her call will receive the Spirit, while those who ignore her calling will suffer loss. Terror and calamity fall upon those who ignore Wisdom.

The Value of Wisdom (2:1–22)

God calls us to listen to His Word and follow His commandments. His Word imparts wisdom and understanding. As we heed God's Word, He delivers us from the brokenness of this world and its evil and adulterous ways. God will guide us to walk in paths of righteousness and faithfulness.

? What promise does Solomon make in verse 2 for those who set their hearts on keeping God's teachings and commandments? Why is it so difficult to trust God in all things? How can you learn to trust Him with all your heart?

Trust in the LORD with All Your Heart (3:1–12)

Solomon encourages his readers to bind the words of the Lord around their necks and write them on their hearts—that is, to carry them around with us at all times. We should trust the Lord with our whole heart and depend on His wisdom rather than trusting in our limited understanding. The Lord disciplines those whom He loves as a loving Father.

Blessed Is the One Who Finds Wisdom (3:13–35)

Finding wisdom is like finding gold, silver, or precious jewels. The Lord in His wisdom created the earth and seas. Solomon reminds us not to lose sight of the wisdom given by God. The chapter concludes with a series of exhortations on dealing honestly and faithfully with neighbors and others.

LINK BETWEEN THE TESTAMENTS

Tree of Life (Proverbs 3:18 → Revelation 22:1–5)

As Solomon explained the bounty of benefits that comes from finding wisdom, he employed imagery that speaks powerfully to the glory and riches of heaven described at the end of John's Revelation. Proverbs 3:18 describes Wisdom as a tree of life, a reward of inestimable value to those who find it.

We've seen the tree of life before in the Garden of Eden, but that's not the last time it appears in the Scriptures. John described it in the last chapter of Revelation when he described the new heavens and the new earth:

> Then the angel showed me the river of the water of life, bright as crystal, flowing from the throne of God and of the Lamb through the middle of the street of the city; also, on either side of the river, the tree of life with its twelve kinds of fruit, yielding its fruit each month. The leaves of the tree were for the healing of the nations. (Revelation 22:1–2)

Here on earth, we lost access to the tree of life as a result of sin. But God gave us another tree of life—the cross of Jesus Christ, through which He has taken away all our sins. God has prepared an even better home for us in heaven, however, and has given us His Word—His Wisdom—to sustain us until He calls us home into life eternal.

CLEAR THE CONFUSION

Why is it important to make your path straight?

Travel in ancient Israel was far from an easy task. The twisted and hilly roads made a journey of any distance in Israel torturous at best, but straightening and leveling roads was extremely expensive and labor intensive. The concept of being able to travel a straight path would seem amazing to Solomon's readers. The importance of straight and level roads was demonstrated centuries later as the Romans developed a system of roads to connect their far-flung territories.

Solomon promises that the Lord will make our paths straight. Satan and his minions may try to turn us aside from the Lord's way, but through our Savior, Jesus, our path to eternal life is made straight.

What great instruction did Solomon receive from David, his father, in verses 3–9? What instruction did you receive from your father? What important direction do you receive from your heavenly Father?

A Father's Wise Instruction (4:1–27)

Solomon speaks as a father urging his son to heed his instruction. He reflects on his own instruction under his father, David. The chapter repeats the theme of listening to and following the wise instruction given by parents. We need to keep our focus on the path God lays out for His people.

SET THE SCENE

Children and Education in the Old Testament

Formal education of children in the biblical era was very different from education today. We know that at least during the time between the Old and New Testaments, fathers were responsible for teaching their sons how to read the Torah starting at age 5. Then at age 10, boys received additional instruction at their local synagogue. These sessions were led by a teacher, and classes met seven days a week. Class sessions were held in the morning and evening with a midday break.

Girls did not attend school. They would receive training in how to care for a household from their mothers. Fathers sometimes instructed their daughters in reading from the Torah. For both boys and girls, education was intended not to support social status but to teach the Torah and the basics of moral living.

In verse 3, Solomon calls the adulteress "a forbidden woman." Why has God forbidden His children to approach such women? How does the powerful lure of internet hookups and pornography weigh into this discussion?

Warning Against Adultery (5:1–23)

The father warns his son against the temptations of an adulterous woman. Such women may offer immediate appeal, but in the long term, they just bring destruction. Rather than succumbing to the temptation of an evil woman, it is better to remain faithful to your wife. She is the one who will bless you with family and remain faithful to you throughout your life.

Practical Warnings (6:1–19)

Solomon offers four practical pieces of wisdom in this section of Proverbs:

(1) Solomon warns against being a cosigner for a neighbor's debt. You should avoid becoming entangled in your neighbor's financial matters.

(2) The ant serves as an example of avoiding laziness. While we need to rest, we also must remain productive.

(3) Dishonest men lie and deceive others; they will face calamity and destruction.

(4) Solomon lists seven behaviors that are an abomination to the Lord.

?

What's the best practical advice you've ever been given? What practical warning would you share with others?

Warnings Against Adultery (6:20–35)

WAYPOINT

What does this text show us?

Once again, these proverbs are addressed from a father to his son. The theme of following the teachings of our father and mother found in chapter 1 is repeated here. They have taught their sons to avoid the ways of an evil woman and their daughters to avoid the ways of evil men.

The temptation of beauty and sinful lust can lead young men and women astray to an unfaithful man or woman. The writer compares sexual sins to playing with fire. Everyone who commits adultery brings ruin on themselves and upon their household.

What does this text reveal about God's plan of salvation?

God designed human society to be built upon the foundation of marriage, one man and one woman united for life. Sexual desire was God's gift to unite husband and wife together and to lead to procreation and the growth of the human family. When Adam and Eve fell, that holy desire became tainted by sin. God laid all our sins of sexual immorality and impurity on His Son, Jesus, when He suffered on the cross, providing us salvation.

What does this text uncover about our identity and calling as God's people today?

The Lord calls His people to faithful living through His Word. Just as parents at the time of Solomon were exhorted to teach their children the basics of the faith and the importance of righteous living, today's parents have the same calling. God desires that we train the next generation in the basics of the faith and what Christ has done in their lives. Through such instruction,

?

This proverb compares fornication, and especially adultery, to what thing that causes unavoidable harm? How can this warning help fortify us against our desires and the temptations the internet parades before our eyes?

?

God sent His Son, Jesus, to die in our place for our sins. What comfort does Jesus offer to people who have destroyed their marriages and lives with sexual sins?

?

After studying this section of Proverbs, what practical advice could you offer to young people facing sexual temptations in the world today?

young people may avoid the self-destruction of sin, learn to guard God's good gift of marital sexuality, and lead faithful and humble lives before God.

LINK BETWEEN THE TESTAMENTS

Warnings Against Adultery → Sexual Immorality (Proverbs 5:1–6:35 → 1 Corinthians 5:1–13; 6:9–20)

The scriptural warning against adultery and its potential consequences in our personal and spiritual lives was certainly not limited to Solomon's writings here in Proverbs. The Sixth Commandment speaks directly to the sin of adultery, and the Mosaic Law spelled out the consequences of sexual sins.

Likewise, Paul addressed the issues of adultery and sexual sin in his letter to the church at Corinth. In 1 Corinthians 5, Paul explained that he had received word concerning sexual sin among the believers in the Corinthian Church. Paul encouraged the people to separate themselves from the sexually immoral. In chapter 6, he went on to spell out additional concerns as he encouraged the faithful to "flee from sexual immorality. Every other sin a person commits is outside the body, but the sexually immoral person sins against his own body" (6:18).

Paul reminds us that we are not our own; through our Baptism, we are united into the very Body of Christ. Christ paid the price for our sins and won our redemption through His suffering, death, and resurrection.

Warnings Against the Adulteress (7:1–27)

Proverbs 1 portrays Wisdom as a woman who stands in the marketplace calling out to anyone who will listen. The rival woman here in Proverbs 7 also stands out in the public square calling to a young man. But the purpose of her cries for attention are quite different from those of Wisdom.

The adulteress desires only to seduce the young man. The consequence of falling for her temptations leads to disaster for the young man. Once again, with a very vivid and memorable proverb, the father reminds his son of the path God has laid out for him and urges him to remain faithful to the Lord.

The Blessings of Wisdom (8:1–36)

WAYPOINT

What does this text show us?

The voice calling to man switches from the adulterous woman to the righteous voice of Wisdom. This voice does not call out to tempt man but rather to speak of "noble things" (v. 6). By wisdom, rulers lead kingdoms; the fruits of wisdom far exceed the wealth of silver or gold. The Lord possessed wisdom at the very beginning, before the mountains and seas were even created. Wisdom calls once again for man to heed her instruction and receive the Lord's favor.

What does this text reveal about God's plan of salvation?

Verse 5 reminds us that all mankind is foolish, born in sin. Wisdom calls all to repent and listen to the voice of the Savior, who is Wisdom personified. Bible scholars suggest that in these verses, Wisdom is actually Christ Himself, who was with the Father before the creation of the world.

Verses 29–31 drives this fact home when Wisdom says, "When He marked out the foundations of the earth, then I was beside Him, like a master workman, and I was daily His delight, rejoicing before Him always, rejoicing in His inhabited world and delighting in the children of man."

Part of Christ's mission in God's plan of salvation was to teach wisdom to mankind. So He spent three years in public ministry, teaching His disciples and followers. His Sermon on the Mount (Matthew 5–7) is an example of the wisdom Jesus taught.

What does this text uncover about our identity and calling as God's people today?

Throughout the book of Proverbs, Wisdom calls the believer to imitate all her ways. In the same way, God calls all mankind to come to Christ and follow Him as disciples through the work of the Spirit in the words of the Scriptures.

?

Review the text in Proverbs 8. Which of the messages from Wisdom in this chapter speak the most strongly to you?

?

Reread Genesis 1 picturing the Son at the right hand of the Father. What phrases from these verses could refer to Jesus rejoicing and delighting as His Father unfolds His divine design of creation day by day?

?

What things in your life make it difficult to follow the wisdom of Christ? How could you grow in your understanding of God's wisdom?

The Way of Wisdom (9:1–12)

Wisdom builds her house and lays out a banquet with the best of everything. She sends out her helpers to invite all to come in. When you attempt to correct the unrighteous, you get nothing in return. However, when you correct a righteous man, he will receive your correction with grace and gratitude.

PICTURE OF THE SAVIOR

"Come, eat of my bread and drink of the wine I have mixed." (Proverbs 9:5)

Among the multitude of wise sayings in King Solomon's collection lies a confirmation of the meal that Christ would institute with His own body and blood. When we receive the Lord's Supper, we are receiving a tangible gift of God's grace that we understand through His promises to us in the Scriptures. We are gladdened by His words because we know what He is saying is true, and in that joyful understanding, we receive spiritual nourishment through the meal each time we participate. Those who are foolish only condemn themselves by eating the meal, as Paul says in Romans 14:23, "because the eating is not from faith." Solomon's words do not merely speak of regular food and sustenance in the abstract. Jesus Christ would give His very body and blood as this gift of great wisdom for believers across time, and these proverbs help us to see the gift that it truly is.

The Way of Folly (9:13–18)

Folly sits outside her door and loudly calls to all who pass by. Instead of offering wine and meat, she offers stolen bread and water—prison fare. Those who fall for her adulterous temptations end up with the rest of her victims in Sheol and ultimately, if they do not repent, in hell.

LINK BETWEEN THE TESTAMENTS

Wise Living → Godly Living (Proverbs 9 → Titus 2:11–15)

In Proverbs 9, Solomon offered a concise summary of the basic principles of wise living. Wisdom invites us in to listen to her message. The wise man, the righteous man, listens to God's instruction and grows in wisdom and understanding.

The grace of God brings salvation to all believers. God's Word gives believers guidance for living as godly people. Through Christ's death and resurrection, He has made us "a people for His own possession" (Titus 2:14).

The Proverbs of Solomon (10:1–22:16)

Solomon's proverbs in this section demonstrate what wisdom and folly look like in practice. They remind us of our own folly, which is rebellion against God that not only leads to bad consequences in this life but will also damn us for all eternity unless we repent and trust in Jesus Christ.

True wisdom flows from trust in the Lord. Most proverbs in this section are two lines long. These contrasting lines instruct us in wisdom.

CLEAR THE CONFUSION

Why are all of these proverbs short and stuffed together? How are they organized?

When studying the book of Proverbs, readers note a distinct shift between chapters 1–9 and chapters 10–22. While both sections begin by stating Solomon's authorship (1:1; 10:1), the style and length of the proverbs differ greatly. The proverbs in the first nine chapters are longer and grouped around definite themes. Suddenly the proverbs shift; most of the proverbs in chapters 10–22 contain only two lines of poetry apiece, and there seems to be little connection between adjacent proverbs. In fact, closer inspection of these proverbs in their original Hebrew reveals connections lost in the translation to English and other languages.

About Sons (10:1–5)

This section of proverbs begins with the contrast between wise and foolish sons. The contrasts continue with other concepts, concluding with a prudent son who gathers in summer and a shameful one who sleeps through harvest.

About the Mouth (10:6–23)

This section contains a number of proverbs concerning the positive or negative use of the mouth. In them, Solomon warns against the incorrect use not only of our mouths but also of our eyes, lips, and so forth. The consequences of misusing speech, or other things mentioned, are dissension and other difficulties.

LINK BETWEEN THE TESTAMENTS

About the Mouth → Taming the Tongue (Proverbs 10:6–23 → James 3:1–12)

A big piece of wisdom in Solomon's proverbs centers around man's tongue. The words we speak can be an instrument of great good for ourselves and others, or they can lead to disastrous evil. Learning to tame and use our tongue well goes a long way as one treads the path of God's wisdom, which is why Solomon highlights it at the beginning of this collection.

This understanding became even more invaluable as the early church grew and developed, and James readily understood the timelessness of Solomon's words. He wrote,

> For every kind of beast and bird, of reptile and sea creature, can be tamed and has been tamed by mankind, but no human being can tame the tongue. It is a restless evil, full of deadly poison. With it we bless our Lord and Father, and with it we curse people who are made in the likeness of God. From the same mouth come blessing and cursing. My brothers, these things ought not to be so. (James 3:7–10)

It remains the case that sin has corrupted even our very speech, often creating discord and chaos where fraternity and magnanimity should persist in the church and in the world. Christ has set us free from our slips of the tongue, so especially today, we ought to seek God's guidance for controlling our tongues for our interactions with fellow believers and nonbelievers alike so that we can be effective witnesses to the Gospel.

Choose one proverb in 10:24–12:12 that really makes a point to you. How does God use His Word to guide us away from wickedness and toward righteousness?

About the Wicked and the Righteous (10:24–12:14)

Seemingly each verse in this section of Proverbs presents a contrast between the behaviors and attitudes of the wicked and the righteous. The pattern varies: sometimes the positive attribute of the righteous is presented, followed by the negative character of the wicked; other times the negative behavior is presented first, followed by the positive. These proverbs could potentially stand alone, but their grouping suggests that Solomon placed them together as a teaching tool.

SET THE SCENE

Understanding Righteousness

Solomon dedicated a good portion of his proverbs to discussing the concept of righteousness. Righteousness can be defined as being morally right or justifiable. Righteousness can be directly contrasted against our sinfulness. In a sermon he preached on Romans 6, Martin Luther compared the two this way:

Freedom from righteousness → Service of sin

Service of righteousness → Freedom from sin

When we abandon righteousness, we serve the cause of sin. When we serve righteousness, we reject sin and its power over us. However, our sinful nature prevents us from being righteous before God. The only righteousness we have comes to us from Jesus Christ, who earned that righteousness through

His perfect life, innocent death, and glorious resurrection. This righteousness becomes ours through faith.

Read through this section again. Which one contrast between wisdom and foolishness stands out for you? Describe an experience in your life (past or present) to which it strongly applies.

About the Wise and Foolish (12:15–15:19)

Solomon continues his theme of wisdom and foolishness regarding the use of our speech. A father urges his son to heed his advice to remain trustworthy. The wise use of wealth, hope, and good sense are key to the life of the faithful. The faithful leave their children a worthwhile inheritance.

The proverbs continue to contrast the wise and simple and the relationship between man and his neighbor. A gentle response prevents conflict. Those who ignore or despise their father's instruction bring destruction upon themselves.

LINK BETWEEN THE TESTAMENTS

A Wise Inheritance → Heirs with Christ (Proverbs 13:22 → Romans 8:12–17)

Moving further into the wisdom of Solomon, a small section about money, inheritances, and family wisdom stands out as a connective feature that helps tie together the Old and New Testaments. Here, Solomon implores us to remember that money and wealth are blessings from God and to value them as such. Fools hoard and cheat to gain much but wind up losing it all very quickly—and finally lose it altogether in death.

Those who seek to obey God, on the other hand, find that what they give back to the Lord in thought, word, and deed builds up their eternal treasure in heaven. The apostle Paul reflected this insight with regard to our greatest possession: faith in Jesus Christ. He writes, "The Spirit Himself bears witness with our spirit that we are children of God, and if children, then heirs—heirs of God and fellow heirs with Christ, provided we suffer with Him in order that we may also be glorified with Him" (Romans 8:16–17). We have been given something more valuable than any riches or precious thing on earth—redemption through Jesus Christ. Wisdom, then, holds our redemption in the highest regard and treasures the faith, which springs from the Gospel, with the utmost care so that we might be able to share the Gospel message freely with the world as Christ Himself has called us to do.

About Men (15:20–16:9)

The wise son is a joy to his parents; he honors the Word of the Lord. The wicked man is far from the Lord and dishonors God. Mankind is pure in its own eyes but far from the Lord. God guides the way of the righteous.

How would it have changed the focus of a king's efforts in biblical times to know he didn't have to establish his throne, because God would do that? What are some practical expectations that God has for faithful leaders today?

About Kings and Leaders (16:10–33)

God establishes the throne of the king. The king honors the righteous and expects the loyalty of his people. By contrast, the deceptive man spreads dishonor and violence. Long life is filled with glory, and being slow to anger is greater than mighty power.

VISUALIZE

"A just balance and scales are the Lord's." (Proverbs 16:11)

About Parents and Children (17:1–6)

A quiet household is a blessing from God. The Lord tests His people, refining them as one purifies silver and gold. Like refining, this testing removes the impurities of our sinful thoughts, words, and deeds and leaves behind pure hearts and minds. God blesses the aged with grandchildren as an inheritance from faithful children.

SET THE SCENE

Family Life

The structure of family life in the Old Testament varied greatly from the lives of families today. Biblical-era families lived in large multigenerational groups headed by a patriarch—typically, the eldest male. The patriarch had the responsibility of training the younger generations in God's laws and the various religious practices of the children of Israel.

Families normally lived in close proximity to other members of their clan—those descended from the same tribe of Israel. Interactions between members of the extended family would occur on a regular basis. Families would gather for religious and other celebrations. Families worked together to care for the flocks, to plant and harvest crops, and to carry out other such activities. Both adults and children would have responsibilities and assigned tasks.

About Foolish Judgment (17:7–24)

The proverbs in this section are connected through a number of examples to illustrate the consequences of foolish behavior. Together, these examples paint a vivid picture of how mankind's sinful choices affect not just ourselves but others as well.

About Fools and Grief (17:25–19:12)

VISUALIZE

"The lot puts an end to quarrels." (Proverbs 18:18)

WAYPOINT

What does this text show us?
The proverbs in this section encourage the reader to avoid fools. Foolishness affects not just the fool but also those around him. Fools would do better to keep silent rather than to speak and reveal their foolishness. When you isolate yourself, you are more easily tempted. The mouth can be a source of trouble and temptation.

The Lord is a source of strength for the righteous man—unlike wealth, which offers no real protection. The proverbs contrast the riches found only in the Lord against the temporary nature of man's pursuits. It is better to be poor and truly wise than to trust in earthly wealth, which fails us.

What does this text reveal about God's plan of salvation?
The writer of these proverbs reminds us repeatedly of the wisdom found in following the Lord's direction. Yet each of us fails to perfectly follow the Lord's direction. God sent His Son, who faithfully called on Him as Lord and perfectly

?

Skim the text once again, and list some of the ways fools demonstrate their foolishness and the wise show their wisdom.

?

How does God demonstrate His plan of salvation in our lives?

honored His Father's direction, earning the righteousness He credits to us in Baptism. The Lord Jesus is a tower of strength and safety for all who call on Him. We depend solely on His salvation, strength, and power. On our own, we are weak and powerless; we can only live in Christ alone.

What has God called you to do in your everyday life to share His Word with others?

What does this text uncover about our identity and calling as God's people today?
God calls believers to be His very own. He invites us to come to Him for grace and forgiveness and for the wisdom and strength to live our lives for Him.

About Foolish Sons (19:13–20:30)

The previous section of Proverbs encourages the reader to avoid fools. The focus in this section shifts, focusing on the reality that everyone will need to deal with fools at some point. The writer then goes on to cite specific examples of the types of fools one encounters, including sons and lazy individuals.

The warnings about dealing with fools continues with additional examples of lazy individuals and how their behavior causes serious consequences. God warns kings to be faithful leaders and sons and daughters to remain faithful to their parents.

VISUALIZE

SET THE SCENE

When is harvest time in Israel? What is the significance of this timing?

The consequences of not planting at the appropriate time affect the harvest and ultimately the supply of food. Planting too early can result in the seed dying and rotting in the cold, wet soil. Planting too late can rob the growing plant of the spring rains it needs. And an early frost can kill the fruit or grain before it has time to ripen. In North America, the majority of crops are planted during the spring (March–May) and harvested in the fall (September–November).

Planting and harvest in Israel works quite differently. Since the majority of their annual precipitation falls between September and April, crops are planted in the late fall and grow through the winter, with harvest occurring in the spring. (This same pattern is typical in the temperate regions of the southern hemisphere.) The harvest was celebrated during the Feast of Firstfruits and the Feast of Weeks. Later this feast became known as Pentecost. Following the resurrection of Jesus, this festival became the day the Father sent the Holy Spirit to all believers.

The Lord's Control over Wise and Foolish (21:1–22:16)

This section of Proverbs spells out the consequences of unrighteous behavior and God's grace and favor shown through His mercy. Note how the verses shift between the actions of the righteous and of the unrighteous. These proverbs clearly outline how riches and poverty affect our lives and our relationship with God. The importance of honoring God through our lives is repeated again and again in this section. "A good name is to be chosen rather than great riches, and favor is better than silver or gold (22:1).

How does the Lord protect us from foolishness? How has He blessed the wise?

LINK BETWEEN THE TESTAMENTS

Train Up a Child → Wise unto Salvation (Proverbs 22:6 → 2 Timothy 3:14–17)

One of Solomon's most well-known and often-quoted proverbs occurs in Proverbs 22:6: "Train up a child in the way he should go; even when he is old he will not depart from it." These words echo God's instruction concerning His Word given to the children of Israel in Deuteronomy 6:6–7: "These words that I command you today shall be on your heart. You shall teach them diligently to your children, and shall talk of them when you sit in your house, and when you walk by the way, and when you lie down, and when you rise."

In the second letter addressed to his spiritual son, Timothy, Paul commended Timothy's family for training up a child. Paul saw in Timothy the result of lifelong faithful instruction in God's Word:

> But as for you, continue in what you have learned and have firmly believed, knowing from whom you learned it and how from childhood you have been acquainted with the sacred writings, which are able to make you wise for salvation through faith in Christ Jesus. All Scripture is breathed out by God and profitable for teaching, for reproof, for correction, and for training in righteousness, that the man of God may be complete, equipped for every good work. (2 Timothy 3:14–17)

Throughout the Scriptures, we see God's desire for His people to study and learn from His Word. As parents, grandparents, and supporting adults, we have God's direction to raise up future generations in the faith with the knowledge of God's Word. Through that Word, we hear the Gospel message of Christ's work of salvation. Through His life, death, and resurrection, we have the promise of eternal life with Him.

CLEAR THE CONFUSION

What happened when I trained up my child as Proverbs 22:6 states and my child fell away from faith? Did God's promise fail?

First, recognize that the book of Proverbs gives observations about life and common outcomes of behaviors, both good and bad. These are not the same as God's promises of forgiveness, life, and salvation through Jesus Christ. Generally speaking, many children who are raised in the faith will remain in the faith. But there are always exceptions. Salvation is a gift of God by grace through faith in Christ by the Word and Sacrament. However, in that state of salvation, your child will be constantly tempted to stop following God and turn away. We cannot choose to be saved, but we can walk away from the faith. There are many, many biblical examples of good and faithful parents who raised their children right but whose children fell away. There are many examples among the kings from the line of David in 1 and 2 Kings and 2 Chronicles. The classic example is the judge Samson, whose parents were careful to instruct him in the Lord (see Judges 13–16). We can also remember Judas. Jesus carefully instructed him as one of His twelve disciples, yet Judas fell away from Christ and ended up betraying Him. Judas's fall was completely his own fault; Jesus didn't do anything wrong.

If this is your situation and your child has turned away from God, don't give up on him. Continue to persistently pray for him and speak to him about

God's promises, especially when he is going through difficulties. Trust God, and commend your child into His loving hands.

Proverbs from Wise People (22:17–24:34)

This section includes proverbs Solomon gathered from other wise authors. Since true piety is not only avoiding evil but also trusting God, Solomon urges us not to envy sinners but to fear the Lord, who has graciously promised us a glorious future for Jesus' sake.

Words of the Wise (22:17–24:22)

Following the introductory verses, the first section (22:22–23:14) focuses on how one should interact with others, including in business and with those of lesser means. Of special interest is 23:13–14, which directs parents to discipline their children and explains the positive results that normally flow from such discipline.

The second half of this section (23:15–24:22) contains seventeen sayings, which could be grouped under the heading of fatherly advice. These proverbs warn the reader against temptations we face in our daily lives.

Review this section again, and identify one or two of the words to the wise you find most helpful. What situations in your life do they address?

CLEAR THE CONFUSION

Does Proverbs 23:13–14 condone child abuse?

"Do not withhold discipline from a child; if you strike him with a rod, he will not die." In our culture, this proverb sounds abusive and cruel. Is God telling us corporal punishment is the only effective way to discipline children?

We should remember God's overall purpose in disciplining us and in having parents discipline their children. His purpose is to teach us and our children to discipline ourselves so that we learn how to restrain our sinful desires and deny ourselves from acting on them to our harm and the harm of others. That is why God told an angry Cain, "Sin is crouching at the door. Its desire is contrary to you, but you must rule over it" (Genesis 4:7).

Since all of us are conceived and born with the sinful nature and all its evil desires, we need our parents to discipline us, to restrain those evil impulses until we are old enough to recognize them as evil and control them ourselves. Parents do not need to resort to physical punishment, but if we fail to teach our children about inappropriate desires and discipline them, they will likely grow up unable to control themselves and will cause great harm to themselves and to others.

What ways did your parents discipline you when you were a child? Why is it important for parents to establish a loving, positive relationship with their children rather than one of fear in order for discipline to be effective?

Sometimes, it is enough to speak firmly to our children. But there are other times when they won't listen and we have to use stronger methods to get their attention. Whatever we choose must always be done from love for our child and an awareness of the harm she will likely do to herself if she doesn't stop.

More Sayings of the Wise (24:23–34)

The writer advises against judging the workmanship of others or being a witness against your neighbor. The fields and vineyards of a lazy or senseless man reveal their ownership by their poor condition.

King Hezekiah ordered his scribes to copy these proverbs especially for kings. Think of the line of descendants who followed Solomon on David's throne, who are chronicled in 1 and 2 Kings and 2 Chronicles, especially noting those who were wicked and those who were faithful. What difference would it have made for Israel if more kings had kept these proverbs in mind?

Solomon's Proverbs Recorded by Hezekiah (25:1–29:27)

Proverbs 25:1 states that the proverbs of Solomon in this section were copied many centuries after his death by King Hezekiah's scribes. Hezekiah saw these proverbs as particularly helpful to guide a king and to advise people about approaching a king. Upon examination, we see that these sayings are organized into four distinct collections: About Kings and Their Courts; About Fools; About Family, Friends, and Others; and About Kings and Rulers.

More Proverbs of Solomon (25:1–29:27)

About Kings and Their Courts (25:1–27)

These proverbs guide the reader in regard to dealing with those who rule over us. Believers should avoid legal action against neighbors. Carefully chosen words have great value. Rulers should exhibit patience when dealing with those under them. We should provide for—and show kindness to—our enemies.

Which is worse in your opinion: a fool or a sluggard? Why?

About Fools (25:28–27:4)

This section begins by making a number of examples of behaviors that apply to fools. Remember that fools are not people with low IQs but rather people who reject God and His wisdom. These statements remind kings not to surround themselves with ungodly men, no matter how intelligent, crafty, or skillful. The proverbs about fools are followed by statements related to dealing with lazy sluggards. The section concludes with a number of statements concerning foolish behavior.

CLEAR THE CONFUSION

What is Proverbs 26:12 saying?

We have just seen eleven verses (26:1–11) pounding away at fools (unbelievers) and why they should not be permitted in the king's presence. Now look closely at verse 12: "Do you see a man who is wise in his own eyes? There is more hope for a fool than for him." It is a brilliant way to make us realize that being wise in our eyes is as bad as being a fool—a realization we may not always have. It makes us stop and examine ourselves to ask, Am I wise in my own eyes?

What does that mean? It refers to someone who is unteachable because she thinks she understands everything and has nothing new to learn—that is, totally unresponsive to God and His Word.

About Family, Friends, and Others (27:5–22)

Relationships with family, friends, and others depend on honest communication and behavior. When we treat others with respect and honor, it means we are willing to gently confront their sins and they ours. This leads each of us to repentance and more godly living. Just as gold and silver are refined, so we will be tested and refined. But such rebuke will not help an unbeliever, for even crushing a fool will not separate foolishness from him.

What practical advice for dealing with family do you find most helpful in this section?

VISUALIZE

"Iron sharpens iron, and one man sharpens another." (Proverbs 27:17)

SET THE SCENE

Refining Gold and Silver

In biblical times, nuggets of gold and silver were often filled with impurities, like bronze, tin, and iron. These impurities are called *dross*. To separate the precious metal from the dross, fire was used. The metals were melted, causing the impurities to float to the surface.

Interestingly, when God refines His children, He often uses fiery trials that expose and remove our sinful desires and bring us in prayer and repentance to Him. But sadly, since a fool is an unbeliever, it is impossible to separate his sin from him no matter what trial he may suffer. Only God can remove the impurity, as the Holy Spirit works repentance and faith through the Word and Sacraments.

PICTURE OF THE SAVIOR

Tested by His Humble Lack of Praise

Solomon's advice regarding interpersonal relations gives us yet another glimpse at the character of Jesus in advance, this time focusing on His great humility. Proverbs 27:21 states, "The crucible is for silver, and the furnace is for gold, and a man is tested by his praise." Solomon proposes that humility is critical when we accept praise from others, and in general, it is best to adopt a humble attitude and not to think ourselves above our station. Humility, as important as it is for us to embody, was one of Jesus Christ's defining characteristics while He walked the earth. He sought no fame or splendor beyond what was necessary for His ministry, and He always directed His followers back to the Scriptures and to the Father in all of His teachings. Most importantly, Jesus humbled Himself by laying down His life upon a cross—a criminal's punishment—so that we would be glorified before God the Father and redeemed for life in heaven with Him. Humility is a powerful gift of the Holy Spirit, and He helps us strive to embody Christ's example of it as we live from day to day.

In what ways could leaders today use this advice as they govern?

About Kings and Rulers (27:23–29:27)

The proverbs in this section encourage shepherds to watch carefully over their flocks. This admonition transitions to directing kings as they rule over their people as a faithful shepherd.

The writer encourages kings to show no partiality between the poor and the wealthy. Any kingdom faces its greatest challenge from wicked people who want to lead the faithful away from God. Wise kings drive the evil from their presence.

Agur's Proverbs (30:1–33)

We do not know the identity of Agur, nor when or where he wrote. His proverbs feature numerical sayings in which he presents a list of items and asks us to guess what each of those items has in common.

The Words of Agur (30:1–33)

Agur's proverbs fall into distinct sections. The first (vv. 1–10) deals with God, His Word, and the church. These verses recount the might and power of God. God's works defy our understanding. His Word is true and everlasting. His promises are to all generations.

The remaining verses (vv. 11–33) deal with our lives in God's kingdom, specifically in relationships with family and civil authorities. Agur reminds readers about the importance of honoring parents and dealing with children. In addition to these relationships, God calls us to deal with kings and other civic leaders.

SET THE SCENE

Who was Agur?

Proverbs 30 cites Agur as the author of the sayings found in this chapter. However, the actual identity of Agur has been lost to history. Jewish tradition says that the name was a pseudonym for Solomon. This appears to be an attempt to credit Solomon as the sole author of the book of Proverbs. But there is no evidence for this tradition.

The name *Agur* may have its roots in one of two Hebrew words, one meaning "to sojourn" and the other "to gather." His name perhaps reflects what he did as the gatherer or assembler of these proverbs. Agur is identified as the "son of Jakeh," who, like his son, is unknown outside of this reference.

King Lemuel's Proverbs and a Poem About an Ideal Wife (31:1–31)

This section begins with words of wisdom that King Lemuel learned from his mother. These words are sound advice for anyone in a position of leadership, including parents. Then it concludes with a wonderful poem that extols the virtues of a faithful Christian wife.

The Words of King Lemuel (31:1–9)

Interestingly, this final chapter of Proverbs begins with words given to King Lemuel from his mother. In this section, she shares godly counsel with her son that truly applies to all leaders.

Her words admonish all leaders to avoid the temptations brought upon them by sexual promiscuity and the abuse of alcohol. Furthermore, she reminds leaders of their role in protecting those who are poor and oppressed.

SET THE SCENE

Who was King Lemuel?

The Bible does not clearly identify King Lemuel, nor does it mention him in any place other than here in Proverbs 31. Some Bible commentators suggest that Lemuel may in fact be a pseudonym for another king, perhaps Hezekiah, but they have no strong evidence to support this supposition. While Lemuel and Hezekiah are not the same person, it seems likely that Lemuel lived sometime after Hezekiah.

Although scholars are unable to confirm Lemuel's exact identity, the message taught to him by his mother and passed along to other leaders is a useful one. This very personal message has important applications for all those in leadership positions.

The Woman Who Fears the LORD (31:10–31)

This final section of Proverbs sings the praises of faithful women. A faithful woman is a blessing to her husband and family. She cares for those in her household and community. Through her acts of kindness, a faithful woman blesses everyone around her.

VISUALIZE

ECCLESIASTES

Welcome to Ecclesiastes

The book of Ecclesiastes offers a sobering look at life on this earth from a man of wisdom and experience. The Preacher, King Solomon, is in his senior years, looking back over a life that to some would seem the best this world has to offer. Solomon had enjoyed great wisdom, fantastic wealth, fame, intricate building projects, and more wives and women than he could keep track of. Yet looking back over it all, he concludes it was all empty, meaningless, in vain.

The book of Ecclesiastes highlights the problems of living for our own desires and pleasures in a world shattered by sin. Solomon shatters the delusion that we have control over our lives and are captains of our own fate. God alone guides our life. One of his favorite phrases is "there is nothing new under the sun"—which silently screams for the coming of the promised Christ and all the new things He will accomplish in His ministry, death, and resurrection.

In our lives, we may not always see God's hand at work amid the turmoil of the world. But in Ecclesiastes, hear wise Solomon teach us to live humbly in a God-fearing manner. With heavenly wisdom, trust God to guide us through the chaos, sin, and inevitable death through which we must pass on our journey to heaven.

?

As you approach this book, what do you already know about Ecclesiastes? What do you hope to learn from elderly Solomon?

Ecclesiastes at a Glance

- **Start:** Solomon introduces himself as "the Preacher" and gives a generally downcast view of the world and what it has to offer. The expression "all is vanity" (v. 2) makes its first, but not final, appearance in the opening chapter of the book. Solomon portrays the pursuits and pleasures of life, as well as any efforts taken under our own power, as fruitless and in vain without God.
- **End:** Ecclesiastes ends with a final reminder to fear God and to remember the judgment that is coming. Only those who live by faith in the promised Christ will receive the reward of eternal life Jesus earned for us all by His life, death, and resurrection.

- **Theme:** Every endeavor we undertake to serve ourselves is foolish and vain. Therefore, take delight in God's power, His ordering of the universe, and His gifts to us, whatever they may be. Our lives are meant to serve God and our neighbor as we look for the second coming of Christ and the restoration of God's eternal kingdom.
- **Author and Date:** King Solomon, also referred to as the Preacher, wrote this work in the last years of his reign.
- **Places Visited:** Like most wisdom literature in the Bible, this book comprises the author's contemplations, prayers, and thoughts. There are no travels or characters, and there are no visions of cities or foreign nations like those we will see in the Books of the Prophets.
- **Journey Time:** These twelve chapters of Solomon's reflections can be read in just over thirty minutes.
- **Outline:**
    - All Is Vanity (1:1–2:26)
    - The March of Time (3:1–4:16)
    - Fear of the Lord and Wisdom (5:1–8:17)
    - Death and Living a Godly Life (9:1–12:14)

Five Top Sights and Spectacles of Ecclesiastes

Ecclesiastes is valuable at any age in life. Why might it be particularly valuable for young Christians?

All Is Vanity (1:1–11) Watch the endless cycles in nature and life and learn that there is nothing new under the sun.

A Time for Everything (3:1–8) Observe how temporal things are always changing as God works out His will in ways we cannot fathom.

The Vanity of Wealth (5:8–6:12) Listen to Solomon's warnings about wealth and the way it can cloud our vision of the world.

Man Cannot Know God's Ways (8:14–17) Notice how unpredictable life is and why it is wiser to live in simple trust in God than to try to anticipate God's workings.

Follow the Commandments of God (12:9–13) Retrace Solomon's steps and learn to repent and submit your will to God in full trust and confidence.

Seeing Jesus in Ecclesiastes

The book of Ecclesiastes focuses on the vanity and misery that come from a lifetime of pursuing our sinful desires and inclinations rather than following God's ways. Solomon tells us of his disenchantment with the pleasures and distractions of this world that we may more clearly understand our need for Jesus, our Savior, who has conquered the sins and woes of this world and promises us eternal pleasures at God's right hand.

All Is Vanity (1:1–2:26)

Solomon relates his efforts to find pleasure, meaning, and delight in the best this world has to offer. He discusses his pursuit of wisdom, pleasure, and grand building projects. But when it dawns on him that he must eventually die and leave it all behind, he realizes the vanity of life without God.

All Is Vanity (1:1–11)

Solomon comes out of the gate swinging with downcast proclamations about the pathetic struggle we endure in an effort to change nature and be remembered for our achievements. Solomon negates all these hopes and dreams with several nature metaphors depicting the futility of change in the face of time: "Around and around goes the wind, and on its circuits the wind returns. All streams run to the sea, but the sea is not full; to the place where the streams flow, there they flow again" (1:6–7). Nothing progresses or provides a lasting impact on the earth, least of all our actions and achievements.

CLEAR THE CONFUSION

What does the phrase "under the sun" (v. 3) mean?

The phrase "nothing new under the sun" (v. 9) is familiar as a proverbial saying. It has its origins in the English translation of this text and in some part captures the attitude projected throughout the book. The phrase implies that the sun is looking down on us, a silent witness of all our life's efforts. But it carries a further implication: a life lived without any consideration of God in heaven above. Solomon used this phrase to describe the life of a fool—a person who says, "There is no god." When Solomon disobeyed God's commandments and pursued his own ways in this world, he was a fool living without God, living "under the sun" without thinking of the God who created it and all things.

?

With the phrase "a generation goes, and a generation comes, but the earth remains forever" (1:4), what is Solomon telling us? What things have made you realize how short our earthly lives really are?

PICTURE OF THE SAVIOR

Is there really "nothing new under the sun" (v. 9)?

The saying was true in Solomon's day and throughout the Old Testament. People were conceived and born in sin and lived under the dominion of sin until they died. God broke in with the covenant of circumcision and the sacrificial system to show that He was calling out a nation for Himself and providing the forgiveness of sins for the sake of the coming Savior.

But truly nothing was new under the sun until the third day, when Christ burst from the tomb. Then something new began—life after death. Through Baptism, you and I have been crucified and are dead to sin, and we have been raised with Christ to new life. When Christ returns to restore His creation, our Baptism will be complete, and we will enjoy eternal pleasures, living forever with our Savior in the new heavens and the new earth, in perfect, glorious, eternal life.

The Vanity of Wisdom (1:12–18)

Solomon, as king, was chiefly known for his God-given wisdom; however, here he decries his gift, for in being wise, he comes to know folly and madness. In knowing and recognizing these things, Solomon sees them more and more often in the world. According to Solomon, those who are wise are cursed by their knowledge: the greater the wisdom, the deeper the despair.

?

Many people dream of things they would do if only they could win the lottery. If money were no object, what would you love to have? What limitations keep you from achieving this? Solomon had no such limitation. What light does his experience shine on the earthly things you desire?

CLEAR THE CONFUSION

What did Solomon mean by saying, "I applied my heart to seek and to search out by wisdom all that is done under heaven" (v. 13)?

Solomon used God's gift of great wisdom to study the various things in the world: philosophy, mathematics, trade, merchandise, mechanics, history, kingdoms, laws, and much more. He also studied self-indulgence—the things many people desire in this world, such as great building projects, accumulating possessions, and pleasures of every kind. Yet Solomon said, "My wisdom remained with me" (2:9). That is, he did not blindly abandon his reason but experimented with these indulgences to see what they really had to offer. His verdict? Vanity. Everything is vanity.

The Vanity of Self-Indulgence (2:1–11)

Along with his wisdom, Solomon was famous for his fabulous wealth, riches that not only extended beyond money but also included wives, slaves, concubines, and everything that was the "delight of the children of man" (v. 8). In this measurement, Solomon was the greatest king of Israel, but he fell victim to the pleasures of this sinful world. His wealth enabled him to pursue everything his heart desired, whether it was pleasing to God or not. Here at the end of his life, Solomon finds that his pursuits had all been meaningless and left no lasting impact on the world around him. They had also failed to improve the condition of his soul.

CLEARING THE CONFUSION

Who are the "children of man" (v. 8)?

The "children of man," or sometimes the "sons of man," is a term used several times not only in Ecclesiastes but also throughout the rest of the Bible. This title refers to all humans, who are descendants of Adam and Eve. Because of Adam and Eve's fall into sin (as told in Genesis 3), each of us has inherited their sinful nature. Thus, throughout the Old Testament, the term "children of man" refers to sinners.

Then Jesus came and made this title new. In the Gospels, Jesus' favorite way to refer to Himself was "the Son of Man." This term not only shows that He is both true God and true man, but it also identifies Him as the Second Adam, the one who will not fall into sin. Through the faith created in us by the Holy Spirit through the Word and Sacraments, Jesus remakes us in His image, holy sons and daughters of man and, more importantly, sons and daughters of God.

LINK BETWEEN THE TESTAMENTS

Vanity of Self-Indulgence → Heavenly Treasure (Ecclesiastes 2:1–11 → Matthew 6:19–24)

The Gospel of Matthew cites Jesus speaking on riches and wealth with these words: "No one can serve two masters, for either he will hate the one and love the other, or he will be devoted to the one and despise the other. You cannot serve God and money" (Matthew 6:24). Solomon warned against pursuing treasures and riches for the purpose of purchasing earthly pleasures. Jesus expanded on this centuries later with the words above and further taught about a heavenly inheritance. In this way, both Testaments remind us to be wary of earthly riches, but Jesus went beyond Solomon, as He proclaimed

?

Wisdom and higher education are goals many parents have for their children. What warning does Solomon offer to those who push their children to higher degrees without giving them a firm foundation in their faith? How can parents prepare their children so higher education will not turn them away from Christ?

that the righteousness of faith on earth will grant an eternal reward far greater than any fortune sinful living could amass in this life.

The Vanity of Living Wisely (2:12–17)

Solomon continues his evaluations by weighing the value of wisdom. In this passage, wisdom appears to be synonymous with virtue or righteousness. So when Solomon declares that it is better to live a life of wisdom, he implies that walking in the ways of God is what makes one wise. Yet Solomon is torn. He wonders if it's worth the effort of such living, because events of good and bad fortune befall both those who live wisely and those who live foolishly. Both the wise and foolish die, and both are forgotten.

The Vanity of Toil (2:18–26)

Solomon describes how he has hated his work and toil. He didn't hate it because of the nature of his work but because he would have to leave all his accomplishments behind to be squandered by another man—in his case, his son Rehoboam. Solomon has a hard time accepting the sentiment of "you can't take it with you." He eventually changes his view, though, and gives us hope, as he decides there is nothing for a man to do but to "find enjoyment in his toil" (v. 24), meaning God's work for him on earth in and of itself should be enjoyed to the best of his ability. We are also called to enjoy the fruits of our labor in our time here rather than storing them up, since they cannot be enjoyed after we die.

Review Solomon's building projects in 1 Kings 7. Why do you think Solomon later came to hate these fabulous buildings? What are some of the cares and worries that come with owning an expensive house, car, or boat? Why must we be wary of seeing our highest delight in our possessions or our work?

CLEAR THE CONFUSION

What became of Solomon's buildings and wealth?

In 2:18–19, Solomon thought of all the buildings he had constructed and all the wealth he had stored up. Then he considered what would happen to these after he died. It is almost as if he knew his son Rehoboam would be foolish and lose all of this wealth and splendor, which is exactly what happened and is recorded for us in 1 Kings 14:25–27. Finally, all of these buildings, including the temple itself, were destroyed by the Babylonians when they conquered Jerusalem and took most of the survivors into captivity (2 Chronicles 36:17–20).

SETTING THE SCENE

Toil and Work from a Biblical Perspective

When God created humans in the Garden of Eden, He appointed them as stewards of His creation. This entailed some form of work, an activity beyond leisure that was pleasing to God and satisfying to man. So why did Solomon find it all meaningless? First, God had put a curse on work when Adam disobeyed His command and ate of the forbidden fruit (see Genesis 3:17–19). The ground was cursed and would no longer yield its strength but instead would yield weeds and thorns. Work of every kind became difficult and wearisome, grinding us down with boredom or repetition; like Solomon, we realize that it is all meaningless because everything we accomplish will one day come to nothing.

Also, work is in danger of becoming a means to an end rather than an end unto itself. We become too focused on stockpiling rewards, money, possessions, recognition, and the like instead of focusing on the joy of our labor as a service to God and our neighbor. Solomon's words warn against this and advise us to keep in mind that the rewards and fruits of our toil are not the paychecks and the things that money can buy. The ultimate happiness of our work comes from the opportunity to serve God by serving our neighbors through the labor of our hands and our minds.

The March of Time (3:1–4:16)

Solomon now turns to a discussion of the short nature of our earthly lives. Things in life often seem chaotic and fickle, as though chance ruled instead of God, but that is only because we do not have God's eternal perspective. The book of Ecclesiastes reminds us that our understanding and perspective are very narrow and limited. We are wise to humble ourselves, to focus on our daily work serving God and our neighbors, and to leave the big questions to God's gracious providence.

A Time for Everything (3:1–8)

WAYPOINT

What does this text show us?

This section of the text is powerful in showing God's divine power and will. Solomon provides us a list of activities and their opposites. These often seem random or even evil as we experience them in life, but Solomon assures us that each is appropriate in its own time. There are times when we are called

?

Describe a time in your life that seemed totally chaotic, like nothing good would ever come of it. Did you eventually see any good resulting from it? What lesson did it teach you about seeking God's help to wait patiently?

to peace and tranquility and other times where we are called to face conflict. There is a time for everything as seen by God, even though we are unable to see the scope of His vision. God knows the times of trouble and of plenty, the hardships and the celebrations—all of it according to His natural order. This reveals in part God's divine ordering of the universe and therefore a divinely appointed time for everything.

Work through each phrase of Ecclesiastes 3:1–8. How did Jesus live through each of these experiences?

What does this text reveal about God's plan of salvation?
Adam and Eve's sin shattered the perfect harmony of God's creation, bringing all kinds of suffering, destruction, war, and chaos. Instead of abandoning His creation and His sinful human creatures, God sent His Son into this world. Jesus experienced everything that is common to human life—times of joy and times of sorrow. He knew hatred, persecution, intense suffering, and even death. Yet in His suffering and death on the cross, Jesus paid the penalty for our sinful rebellion. In His resurrection, He opened to us the door to eternal life. Even now, He sits at the right hand of God the Father, interceding for us and controlling all things in heaven and on earth for the benefit of His believers and His church's mission to continue calling sinners to faith through the Gospel.

Think of a memorable time in your life, good or bad. How does reminding yourself of Jesus' return help you process times like this in your life?

What does this text uncover about our identity and calling as God's people today?
We as God's people are to submit to His ordering of the universe with gladness despite the times of trial and tribulation. In fact, this mindset calls us back to the book of Job. God orders the universe in ways that are beyond our comprehension. When we experience suffering and trials we cannot understand, God would have us focus our thoughts on our Lord Jesus hanging on His cross. There we see God's power to turn sin to righteousness, death to life, hell to heaven. Like Job, and like Solomon, we are called to trust that our gracious, loving heavenly Father has placed us within His established order. Thus, there is a time for everything.

LINK BETWEEN THE TESTAMENTS

A Time for Everything → All Things Work Together for Good (Ecclesiastes 3:1–8 → Romans 8:18–39)

Solomon's list of opposites shows us there is an order and a purpose for all the things that happen in our lives—and that God is in control.

In Romans 8, the apostle Paul gives us an assurance that God is not careless or unaware when troubles and heartbreak strike us. The Holy Spirit helps us in our weakness, interceding for us. God the Father carefully controls the things that happen in our lives, working all together for our good. And Jesus Christ sits at His Father's right hand interceding for us.

How does knowing that Jesus and the Holy Spirit intercede for you and that God the Father makes all things work together give you comfort and peace when you go through difficult times?

CLEAR THE CONFUSION

What good can God work from the bad times in our lives?

God often uses the struggles and hardships in our lives to expose our weakness and drive us into His all-powerful arms. He breaks our self-confidence and teaches us to trust in Him alone. He strengthens the steadfastness of our faith so that we can endure even greater trials that will likewise drive us to despair of our own strength and to fall before Him in prayer. These trials help break our attachment to this fleeting world and prepare us for the hour of death, when Christ will deliver us from this world and all sin and bring us to our glorious eternal home.

The God-Given Task (3:9–15)

Several ideas from earlier in this book are brought together in this section. Taking enjoyment and fulfillment in the work the Lord has provided us is one such idea, but this is also coupled with our place in God's order and enduring under our toil. For God's work is assured, and His plan expands beyond the scope of our earthly vision. God is eternal, and although the idea of eternity is lodged in our hearts, our life on this earth is brief and our understanding is small. Therefore, we are not able to grasp how every incident in our lives fits into the full vision of God's plan. We are left to trust in the Lord and be content with what He has revealed to us and established for us in the here and now.

CLEAR THE CONFUSION

What did Solomon mean when he said, "He has made everything beautiful in its time" (v. 11)?

The Hebrew word translated "beautiful" also means "right" or "fitting." Every living thing and every task God assigns to us has its proper time and place. But since time passes, a time will come when that beauty will pass. Whether that is our physical beauty or strength, our relationships with others, or our jobs, we can trust that when one phase of our lives ends and another begins, God has determined all things and will be by our side to guide us with grace, forgiveness, and blessing. We should not resent or fight against these changes but pray for God's peace and rejoice in His tender care.

From Dust to Dust (3:16–22)

Here we have a shift in tone as Solomon adapts his theme of vanity. The Preacher says that righteousness and justice are overpowered or perforated by evil and wickedness throughout life. He makes specific reference to the children of man, meaning the unbelieving descendants of Adam and Eve who refuse to submit to God's will, and prays they will recognize themselves and their actions as wicked before their day of judgment before Christ comes. For the wicked and the righteous both share the same earthly end: the return to dust like all the animals. As a concluding note to this section, Solomon again emphasizes the thought that we should remain content within our work and position in life, because we are powerless to change it in any meaningful way.

?

What would you say to someone who says there is no sense in serving God because unbelievers do just as well in life as believers and we all end up dying anyway?

CLEAR THE CONFUSION

What did Solomon mean by saying, "In the place of justice, even there was wickedness, and in the place of righteousness, even there was wickedness" (v. 16)?

The place of justice in Israel was the throne of the king and the officials who were judges over Israel. This would be the governmental leaders today. These leaders were to judge with righteousness, punishing the guilty and protecting the innocent. Yet as the history of Israel and Judah showed, many kings were wicked, denying justice to the poor and needy and failing to punish the sins of the rich and powerful.

The place of righteousness was the religious courts, where all judgments should have been made according to God's laws. Today this would be the judges, juries, and courtrooms. The greatest example of wickedness in the Jewish religious courts was when God's Son, Jesus of Nazareth, was brought to trial before the Jewish high court, the Sanhedrin. The high priest summoned an illegal night trial, sought false witnesses, and unjustly sought the death of the innocent Son of God. When Pilate was about to set Jesus free, the chief priests convinced the crowds to demand Barabbas be freed and to cry out repeatedly for Jesus to be crucified.

Evil Under the Sun (4:1–16)

?

Consider a time in your life when you were most gripped by rivalry and envy. Looking back now, how does that response feel to you?

Solomon recognizes the oppression in the world and the abuse of power that his kingly peers, and even he himself, have perpetrated on those under them. It is so heinous to him, though, that he views those who have died or who have not yet been born as more fortunate than anyone living.

Furthermore, Solomon analyzes the rivalry and envy that so often drive us to compete against one another. He recognizes that our struggles against one another bear nothing but poisonous fruit. The solution, according to Solomon, is to come together and ease one another's burdens. Lastly, Solomon moves back to his own legacy and perspective as king. He suggests that it would be better to be unknown, poor, but wise than rich, of high station, but foolish—for the wise overtake the foolish. He qualifies this last statement, though, by reminding us that even the wisest kings are forgotten.

LINK BETWEEN THE TESTAMENTS

Support One Another → Bear One Another's Burdens (Ecclesiastes 4:9–12 → Galatians 6:1–2)

While Solomon wrote about the physical and earthly burdens that are inflicted upon us and how we should support one another in our endeavors, the apostle Paul took similar language to address burdens of a spiritual nature. Paul was, of course, concerned with bodily struggles and so encouraged support as proclaimed by Jesus for His disciples to love their neighbors (everyone), but the focus in this particular section of Galatians is on spiritual burdens, specifically burdens that deal with temptations and the worldly pull of sin. We are called by God to look after one another in body and mind, with concern not just for our health but for our souls as well. Both Paul and Solomon guide us to bear one another's weight in both earthly and spiritual senses, for that is one of the defining points of Christianity.

CLEAR THE CONFUSION

How did Solomon clarify this saying: "There is nothing better than that a man should rejoice in his work, for that is his lot" (3:22)?

In 4:4–8, Solomon teaches us how to examine our attitude toward work so that we may be able to truly rejoice in our work.

First, he counsels us against working out of envy—that is, only working because we are not content with the possessions God has given us but want the things our neighbor has. Then, he warns against toiling too hard at work so that we only end up wearing ourselves out and making ourselves miserable, especially when the reason for that excessive work is our desire to gain wealth or show we are better than our neighbor.

The only way to really rejoice in our work is to be content with the things God provides through that work and to focus on using our time, talent, and energies to serve God as we serve our neighbors.

Fear of the Lord and Wisdom (5:1–8:17)

Solomon now examines fearing God, the vanity of wealth and honor that dominates so many people's lives, and the contrast between wisdom and folly. He reminds people to obey the king's command, remembering that God places the king in this position. He rounds out this section with a reminder to fear and serve God because we cannot know God's ways.

Fear God (5:1–7)

Solomon cautions us against superficial worship. We need to be mindful when we approach the Lord, especially in worship. God takes no pleasure in mindless or hypocritical worship, whether we sit and warm a pew while our heart and mind are elsewhere or if we are secretly cherishing sin in our hearts. We should also be careful to keep the vows we make before the Lord, especially our vows made at Confirmation to be faithful to the Lord and suffer all, even death, rather than fall away from Him and the vows we take at our wedding to forsake all others and love and cherish our spouse until God separates us in death. Solomon concludes we ought to fear the Lord and approach Him with respect and caution. Or, as Luther taught in his explanation of the Third Commandment, "We . . . [should] not despise preaching and His Word, but hold it sacred and gladly hear and learn it."

How easily do you find yourself distracted in worship? What are some ways to push away those distractions?

The Vanity of Wealth and Honor (5:8–6:12)

WAYPOINT

What does this text show us?
Echoes of the previous sections are found within this passage as Solomon once again warns against the dangers of pursuing wealth as the chief goal of our work and toil. If our chief aim is to achieve wealth, then that work is fruitless, for at the end of our life, all our riches will lie dust-covered, useless to us. Therefore, we ought to take joy in our work and toil because it comes from God and serves Him and our neighbors. We do not look to our work to provide for or to accumulate wealth for ourselves. We look to God to supply our needs and look to our work to serve God by meeting our neighbors' needs.

What does this text reveal about God's plan of salvation?
Jesus taught, "You cannot serve God and money" (Matthew 6:24). This passage reminds us of the vanity of pursuing wealth and possessions as if acquiring them would bring us lasting joy and rest. One day, each of us will

What difference does it make whether you work for yourself or work for God and for others, such as your employer, your family, and the people who will benefit from the goods or services you make or offer?

How did Jesus use His God-given gifts to serve the people around Him?

die and stand before God's judgment seat. But God has sent His Son, Jesus Christ, to redeem our souls from sin and death by His death on the cross. For Jesus' sake, we are assured of eternal life in the glorious presence of God. As we look in joyful hope to that future, we can endure the difficulties of life on earth, content that for Jesus' sake, our heavenly Father will provide for all our needs. That enables us to find great joy in serving our neighbors with the work of our hands.

What does this text uncover about our identity and calling as God's people today?

Our calling is to take joy in God's creation, in our work, and in the blessings He has provided to us. We are to give up the illusion of control in our lives and recognize that through Him all proper things come to fruition. This passage demands our trust in God and that we let go of our own power—for only then can we be truly free.

How easy is it for you to give up the illusion of control in your life? Describe a time you let go of that control and experienced the true freedom of trusting God.

LINK BETWEEN THE TESTAMENTS

The Vanity of Wealth → The Parable of the Rich Fool (Ecclesiastes 6:1–2 → Luke 12:16–21)

To warn against sacrificing our relationship with God to pursue wealth, Solomon spoke of a man who lacked nothing of all that he desired. God gave him wealth, possessions, and honor. Yet before he could enjoy these, he died and left them to a stranger to enjoy.

When Jesus was approached by a man who was not content with his share of his father's inheritance, which his brother had divided with him, Jesus told the parable of the rich fool to impress upon him the lesson Solomon gave here.

The difference between Jesus' words and those of Solomon is that Solomon kept an earthly perspective following the man's death—who would enjoy what he left behind? Jesus leads us in a much more important direction. What happens to the man himself after he dies? He must stand before God for judgment. God calls him a fool because his only concern was earthly things, not his relationship with God. Our eternal soul and our eternal destiny are much more important than our bank account or stock holdings. Both Solomon and Jesus call us to repent of our love of wealth and to find peace with God through Jesus Christ, our Savior.

The Contrast of Wisdom and Folly (7:1–29)

In this chapter, Solomon contrasts wisdom with folly, calling us to turn from our sins, repent, and depend on God for our salvation. He directs us to the house of mourning rather than the house of mirth. He teaches us to be patient and wait for God to act rather than lashing out in anger at those who anger us. He cautions us not to think more highly of ourselves than we ought or to fall into the trap of self-righteousness.

One of the bad qualities of our sinful nature is the way it makes us self-righteous. Does that tendency show itself in you more through feelings of superiority over others or justifying your actions to others? Why is it so difficult for us to truly humble ourselves before God and other people?

CLEAR THE CONFUSION

How can someone be too righteous?

This text describes people who think they are so holy they have no need to repent. A good example of this would be the Pharisees in the New Testament, whose pride in their religious observances and their place within the Israelite religious community blinded them to their own sins and the truth that Jesus spoke. Solomon calls us to admit our tendency to be self-righteous and our inability to stop sinning. Solomon repeats this again in verse 20: "Surely there is not a righteous man on earth who does good and never sins." This knowledge drives us to repent and look to God, who is the only provider of our salvation.

Keep the King's Command (8:1–9)

Solomon is commanding people to adhere to the authorities that God has placed over them. The laws of the land and the kings—or in our day and age, presidents and legislators—have been placed over us through God's design, and therefore, we are to serve and obey them so long as they do not command us to disobey God.

LINK BETWEEN THE TESTAMENTS

Keep the King's Command → Paying Taxes to Caesar (Ecclesiastes 8:1–9 → Matthew 22:15–22)

Solomon spoke about respecting the authorities who have been placed over us. Jesus advanced this point in Matthew's Gospel. Jesus was confronted by the Pharisees, who, hoping to trick Him, asked if it was lawful to pay taxes to Caesar. This loaded question served as a trap, for if Jesus answered no, they could have Him arrested for insurrection, but if He answered yes, He would be seen as supporting the Romans and thus despised (they hoped) by His followers.

But Jesus' answer left them simultaneously frustrated and amazed. Taking up a denarius, He asked them to identify whose likeness and inscription was on the coin. They in turn replied that it was Caesar's likeness, prompting Jesus to say, "Therefore render to Caesar the things that are Caesar's, and to God the things that are God's" (Matthew 22:21). This response foiled the Pharisees' trap as He not only agreed with Solomon's statement regarding authority but also placed God as the higher authority, who demands more than coins as a sign of loyalty. We are called by God to adhere to those authorities He has placed over us and to render unto them what is theirs, meaning taxes, loyalty, and service. Such is our vocation as citizens.

CLEAR THE CONFUSION

What is Solomon writing about in 8:8?

Solomon begins this verse by saying, "No man has power to retain the spirit," which refers to the moment of death, when our spirit or breath leaves our body. None of us can lengthen life beyond the time set by God. Solomon continues, "or power over the day of death." This means none of us have the right to shorten our lives by suicide. That, of course, flies in the face of our culture's claims that we have the right to "death with dignity." But suicide is a sin against God, our Father and provider.

Solomon next says, "There is no discharge from war"—that is, the spiritual war between God and Satan, between believer and unbeliever, between our sinful nature and the new creature God has made in us. That spiritual war will not cease until we are freed in death, or until Christ Jesus returns. Finally, Solomon writes, "Nor will wickedness deliver those who are given to it." This is a stern warning to us that we must never surrender the battle to sin, Satan, and wickedness, thinking we have the strength to return to God whenever we choose. God will judge the sinful. Only with His grace through His Son, Jesus Christ, can we be delivered. Therefore, Solomon calls on us daily to repent and turn to Jesus, our only Savior.

?

What is the appeal of "death with dignity," or seeking doctor-assisted suicide? How is it another of Satan's deceitful lies?

Those Who Fear God Will Do Well (8:10–13)

Here Solomon urges us to remain in the ways of God even though it seems there is no immediate or earthly benefit. The wicked may prosper and extend their life by means of their wickedness, but it is in vain because death is inevitable; those who practice evil throughout their life must face God just as those who have followed His commandments and kept His ways must face Him. On that day, the just and righteous will remain and the wicked will be cast into hell. So when Solomon says those who fear God will do well, he means it in a spiritual and heavenly sense: their fortune will not be that of condemned unbelievers.

The Romans believed in swift punishment as the best way to deter others from committing crimes. Over each condemned criminal, they placed a title identifying that criminal and the crime for which he was being punished. In Jesus' case, He was identified as Jesus of Nazareth, punished for being King of the Jews. What are your thoughts about swift punishment? How is it a sign of God's mercy and patience that we are not swiftly punished for our sins?

SET THE SCENE

Swift Punishment?

Solomon made a keen observation: "Because the sentence against an evil deed is not executed speedily, the heart of the children of man is fully set to do evil" (v. 11). That may have been what Adam and Eve first thought when they ate the forbidden fruit. Earlier, God had warned Adam, "In the day that you eat of it you shall surely die" (Genesis 2:17). But when Adam and Eve ate the fruit, they did not die but lived to raise many generations.

That delay of the sentence of death could have convinced them that God was lying and Satan was truthful because the serpent had said, "You will not surely die" (Genesis 3:4). But God's warning was true. In the day they ate that fruit, they suffered a spiritual death far worse than physical death. They lost the ability to fear, love, and trust in God above all things. The punishment for their sin was not just physical death but the eternal death of the fires of hell.

The delay between sin and punishment we experience in our earthly lives can appear to be indecision on God's part, as though He will never punish evildoers. This seeming lack of consequences has convinced others that God does not exist and that there will never be a punishment, just death and nothing more. So Solomon is right: "The heart of the children of man is fully set to do evil."

However, God is patient not because He isn't serious about sin but because He is serious about saving sinners. He is so serious about sin that He punished His Son in our place on the cross. God our Creator does not delight in the death of sinners but desires that they turn from their evil ways and live. When sinners fail to repent, it is their fault alone, never God's.

Man Cannot Know God's Ways (8:14–17)

Solomon seeks to instill in us once more that control of our lives and the events that occur within them is not ours. Instead, the Lord has ordered our lives according to His purpose and has done so in such a way that even the most discerning among us, even the most sage people, cannot see His design perfectly. Instead of spending our lives asking God why, the best thing we can do is trust Him, be content with our work and our present situation, and strive to follow God's path, whatever that may be.

Death and Living a Godly Life (9:1–12:14)

Solomon closes the book of Ecclesiastes with a reminder that death comes to all; therefore, we do well to enjoy life with the people God has brought to us. He speaks of wisdom and how it is much better than folly, even though wisdom cannot keep us from death. Solomon encourages us to be generous when we have the opportunity, for one day we may need the generosity of others. Finally, Solomon poetically speaks of the hardship of growing old, death, and our spirit returning to God who gave it.

Death Comes to All (9:1–6)

This passage is interesting for a number of reasons; chief among them is that Solomon's attitude toward death seems to change. While he has previously stated that the dead have it better than the living (because they are no longer afflicted by the wickedness and suffering of the world), he switches his view here. Now he reminds us the living have the opportunity to learn from the deaths of others, to return to the Lord their Creator, and to help others.

?

What events in your life have made you think about the inevitability of your own death? What lasting effect do those moments bring?

CLEAR THE CONFUSION

What is "the same event" that happens to all people (v. 2)?

Solomon wants to build suspense, so he speaks about this event without directly identifying it. He makes us ask the question, What is this event that happens to both the righteous and the wicked, the good and the evil, the clean and the unclean? Finally, after we have seen the wickedness of the children of man, Solomon answers our question: that event is death.

Enjoy Life with the One You Love (9:7–10)

The sentiment in this passage is lovely, as Solomon encourages us to live in faith and to enjoy the peace of God's forgiveness and the blessings He so freely showers on us in this life. He encourages us to be merry, to find joy in the work and blessings the Lord has given, and to spend life with our spouse. The significance of the singular wife here is astonishing, especially considering Solomon had seven hundred wives in addition to his three hundred concubines. It is as though he was telling us he would have been much happier if he would have been married to only one wife. Regardless, the message proclaiming a love for one person and contentment with our lot in life remains.

Wisdom Better than Folly (9:11–10:20)

Throughout the book of Ecclesiastes, Solomon has struggled with the question of wisdom and whether it is a gift or a curse. The biggest issue he finds is that misfortune and disaster befall the wise just as much as fools. Everything happens according to God's order but looks like chance to us, so there doesn't seem to be any benefit to being wise but only a greater capacity to discern the misery of the world. Solomon, however, finally finds a use for wisdom here and expresses his sentiments in a short story.

The Preacher recounts the time a small city was besieged by a great force with mighty siege engines and war machines. Within the city was a poor, aged, yet wise man who, by his wisdom and counsel, was able to deliver the city from the siege. Unfortunately, after the siege was lifted, his name was forgotten and no one remembered his deeds. The man achieved no personal gain or renown, but Solomon maintains that it would be better to be this despised wise man than a foolish king. (Consider the wise woman in 2 Samuel 20:16–22 whose wisdom saved her city from David's nephew Joab).

How important is it for you to be recognized for the good things you do? Why might it be better to be forgotten by people, knowing your deeds of faith are all remembered by God?

The answer to this puzzle lies in a change of perspective. No, the old man didn't achieve any personal renown, so what did he truly accomplish? For himself, nothing, but for others, everything. He delivered his neighbors from the trials and dangers they faced, and he asked no reward. The wisdom of the old man saved his people from affliction and death. Solomon's point at last stands clear: wisdom is vain if used to pursue personal gain, but when used in service to others, it becomes invaluable and pleasing to God. We are likewise called to apply our gifts to help others in the seemingly random trials and tribulations of life.

CLEAR THE CONFUSION

Was Solomon talking about fate when he said, "Time and chance happen to them all" (9:11)?

Solomon had made this point before. From our earthly perspective, life seems totally random and out of control because it doesn't go as we expect it. Believers suffer loss while the wicked enjoy prosperity. One moment, life is going well; the next, a huge disaster strikes.

But Solomon was not talking about fate or destiny or even blind luck. He had told us before that God is in control, but no matter how wise we are, we cannot guess God's next move or know why He chooses to permit times of good or evil to strike, as Job learned. So why does God permit the troubles in our lives to strike so randomly? He does so to remind us of His coming judgment and to prepare us by using these times to drive us to Him in repentance and faith. Living by faith, we can trust God's promise to make everything in our lives work together for our good, and we can enjoy the blessings He gives as we await the day He will bring us into His glorious presence forevermore.

Cast Your Bread upon the Waters (11:1–10)

Solomon, after his revelation on the purpose of wisdom and his acceptance of the random patterns of life, advises us to take risks, be generous, and live life free from the petrifying effects of absolute doubt and fear. We are to accept God as the continuous authority of the universe, who promises to provide for our every need of body and soul. Ordering our lives accordingly and rejoicing in the life He gives and preserves for us, we must also temper such joy with the recognition of our own darkness and sinful nature.

What do you think is the right balance between hoarding your possessions and giving them away recklessly? How can we learn to live by trusting our God's providence and generosity?

CLEAR THE CONFUSION

What did Solomon mean by "cast your bread upon the waters" (v. 1) and "give a portion to seven, or even to eight" (v. 2)?

By the phrase "cast your bread upon the waters," Solomon referred to the way he would load trade goods onto ships and send them off. He had to wait three years for the ships to return, but they did so loaded down with tremendous profits (see 1 Kings 10:22). Thus, he was referring to sending away some of the daily bread God provides to you as an investment to help others improve their lives, rather than hoarding it and clinging to it for fear of falling into hard times—which would be failing to trust God to provide for your needs.

Giving a portion to seven or eight is similar. It means giving of our daily bread to help meet the needs of others, whether that be food, clothing, or money. Solomon encourages us to give generously to those in need around us, trusting that God will provide for us if we should fall into need, maybe even through those very people we have helped.

Remember Your Creator in Your Youth (12:1–8)

WAYPOINT

What does this text show us?

This passage's powerful poetry illustrates our ever-increasing battle with old age—a battle that increases in its intensity throughout our lives, a battle that we will all lose one day. Time marches on and diminishes our capacity for taking pleasure and joy in all God has called us to do. Solomon warns us that we will fall victim not only to the physical ailments of age but also to a mentality that will make it harder to fear and love God. Therefore, he urges us while still in our youth to remember our Creator by coming to worship each week to receive His gifts through Word and Sacraments. God will sustain us and enable us to endure the last struggling years of life with this strong, living faith.

What does this text reveal about God's plan of salvation?

Back in the Garden of Eden, God had warned Adam that the day he ate of the fruit of the tree of the knowledge of good and evil he would surely die (Genesis 2:17). When we reach the last days of our lives as Solomon describes them here, we know that the day of death and judgment is drawing near.

But even in the garden after Adam and Eve's fall, God promised a Savior. Jesus took our sin and guilt upon Himself and suffered the torment of body and spirit that we deserve throughout all eternity as He suffered and died in our place on the cross. Though we must still suffer death, through Christ Jesus, the door of heaven stands open, and when our final day comes, His promise to the thief at His side will be His promise to us: "Today you will be with Me in paradise" (Luke 23:43).

What does this text uncover about our identity and calling as God's people today?

Whatever our age, it is never too late to come to the Lord in repentance to receive His grace, forgiveness, and peace. Through weekly worship, we are strengthened, especially for the last years of our lives, when our health fails and many people grow bitter and forsake faith. Solomon offers a glimpse of hope that even when the dust (our body) returns to the earth, our spirit will return to the hand of God our Creator, who joined it to our body in our mother's womb. Then when Christ returns, He will raise our lowly bodies and transform them to glorious, eternal bodies. Our spirit will return to our body, and we will live with Him in the new heaven and the new earth forever.

This also reinforces the importance of bringing up our children in the faith through regular church attendance, home devotions, and talking about

?

What health struggles have you had in the past or do you have currently that remind you this earthly life will not last forever? How do you keep these difficulties in a proper perspective?

?

In Jesus' suffering, He experienced much of what Solomon describes here. He grew too weak to carry His cross, and He was helpless to get a drink to quench His thirst. What does such weakness reveal about the amazing love of the almighty Son of God?

?

Consider an activity you are no longer able to do because of age or, if you are younger, an illness or injury that knocked you flat and kept you from being able to do normal activities. What internal struggles does such a condition bring on you? In light of this, how does it help to remember Jesus "has borne our griefs and carried our sorrows" on the cross (Isaiah 53:4)?

our Lord and Savior. Our children can build on this foundation in their adult lives, and Christ will guard them in the faith when they reach their final years.

CLEAR THE CONFUSION

What are the images Solomon used to describe the ailments of old age (vv. 3–6)?

As in the parables Jesus told, Solomon used earthly images to powerfully portray our failing health as death draws near in our older years of life.

- "The keepers of the house tremble" can refer to arms or legs trembling.
- "The strong men are bent" can be bent legs or a bent back.
- "The grinders cease because they are few" are teeth.
- "Those who look through the windows" could be darkened teeth or failing eyesight.
- "Afraid . . . of what is high" is likely the fear of falling and broken hips.
- The moment of death is described with four quick images of sudden destruction: a snapped silver cord, a broken golden bowl, a shattered pitcher, and a wheel broken on an overloaded cart.

But then Solomon offers a glimpse of hope as the body returns to the earth from which it was taken and the spirit returns to the hand of the Creator who made it. In Christ Jesus, we have the promise that the body will be raised immortal and our spirit reunited in eternal life.

Fear God and Keep His Commandments (12:9–14)

Solomon concludes this book with a culmination of all his sentiments. He now has explored the uses and detriments of wisdom, worry, toil, and riches while grappling with the fact that God has control over his life and its course. Solomon ends his tenure as the Preacher and encourages us to keep everything he has contemplated in mind as we follow God's commands and revere Him with fear and awe as the principal authority and director of our lives.

THE SONG OF SOLOMON

Welcome to the Song of Solomon

The Song of Solomon, also called the Song of Songs, expounds on the topics of love and marriage. King Solomon describes his courtship, wedding, and consummation with his beloved bride, a young Shulammite woman.

The Song of Solomon does not provide a linear narrative of Solomon's courtship and marriage to his beloved; instead, it leads us in a beautiful poetic journey through the wonders of love and marriage. Ultimately, this poetry guides us to understand the love Christ shows for His Bride, the church—that is, each of us believers.

As you read the Song of Solomon, contemplate the precious gift of sexual love God has given to be enjoyed within the boundaries of marriage. But even more, consider the intense love that drove God to send His Son for you and Jesus to lay down His life for you.

Why do you think God would inspire Solomon to write a book about marriage to include in the Bible?

The Song of Solomon at a Glance

- **Start:** The Song of Solomon begins with the courtship, wedding, and consummation of the bride and groom.
- **End:** The Song of Solomon ends with a discussion of marital love and an appeal for purity and faithfulness.
- **Theme:** The love story of Solomon and his beloved reminds us of Jesus' love for His Bride, the church.
- **Author and Date:** Solomon, the king of Israel, wrote the Song of Solomon in the early years of his reign (around 970 BC).
- **Places Visited:** Jerusalem, Shunem, Lebanon, sites throughout Israel, the bride's bedchamber, the garden, Solomon's vineyard
- **Journey Time:** The eight chapters of the Song of Solomon can be read in about twenty minutes.

Compare the introductions of the Song of Solomon and Hosea. How does the imagery of marriage change, and how do both describe our relationship with God?

- **Outline:**
  - The Marriage Union in Four Cycles (1:1–5:1)
  - The Reunion in Married Love (5:2–8:14)

Five Top Sights and Spectacles of the Song of Solomon

The Rose of Sharon (2:1–6) Bask in the beautiful imagery of Solomon's poetry as he and his beloved delight in each other.

Awakening Love (2:7; 3:5; 8:4) Listen to the message of the Song of Solomon's repeated chorus: sexual love is pleasing, but we should reserve it for its proper time within marriage.

Solomon Arrives for the Wedding (3:6–11) Celebrate with the daughters of Zion as King Solomon journeys to his bride's house in a traditional Jewish wedding procession.

Set Me as a Seal (8:6–7) Behold the passion and steadfastness of love as Solomon declares that love cannot be conquered by any power, not even death.

Protecting the Little Sister (8:8–9) Witness the care and diligence of older brothers as they protect their younger sister's dignity until she is married.

Seeing Jesus in the Song of Solomon

The Song of Solomon describes the courtship and wedding of Solomon and his beloved. In courtship, Solomon and his beloved delight in each other and prepare for marriage. Then, in the wedding, they are united in marriage and the two become one flesh.

The New Testament teaches that the church is Jesus' Bride. Jesus spoke in marital language during His earthly ministry, promising that He was going to prepare a place for us, just as an Israelite groom would prepare a house for his bride before their wedding.

Christ and the church eagerly await the wedding day, the Last Day, when Christ will return and bring His glorified Bride to the new creation, where we will live together in eternal love.

?

In what ways does the relationship between a bride and groom describe the relationship between the church and Christ?

The Marriage Union in Four Cycles (1:1–5:1)

The first four chapters of the Song of Solomon (plus one verse) unveil the love Solomon and his bride have for each other as they delight in each other through their courtship, their wedding, and its consummation.

The Bride Confesses Her Love (1:1–7)

The Song of Solomon opens with the speech of Solomon's beloved, as she yearns for the consummation of her marriage with Solomon. As she addresses her audience, the daughters of Jerusalem, she remarks on her dark, suntanned skin, which is beautiful.

CLEAR THE CONFUSION

What was the significance of the bride's dark skin?

In ancient Israel, wealthy people from the higher classes had lighter skin because they were protected from the sun. People in the lower classes of society had dark, suntanned skin because they labored outside. The bride in the Song of Solomon is a keeper of vineyards and herder of goats (1:8). This shows she belonged to a lower social class, one that could hardly be expected to receive the attention of the great King Solomon, let alone become his beloved wife. Yet Solomon's own father, David, had been a poor shepherd when God chose him to be king of Israel.

Likewise, each of us believers is a sinner, completely undeserving of God's attention, let alone His favor, mercy, and grace. Yet God's own Son, Jesus Christ, delights in us so much He took on human nature and was born among us. He was born in poverty and laid in a manger for His crib. Jesus shared our earthly life to save us from our sins by His suffering, death, and resurrection. Now, seated at the right hand of God the Father in great glory, He guards and guides us as we await the day of His return, when we will rule the new creation at His side.

Solomon and His Bride Delight in Each Other (1:8–2:7)

What experiences have you had with eagerly anticipating an approaching wedding?

How does the imagery of marriage help us better grasp the relationship Jesus has restored between sinners and God through His life, death, and resurrection?

What are some ways to avoid stirring up desire or awakening love before its appropriate time?

WAYPOINT

What does this text show us?

Solomon enters the poem as he and his beloved prepare for their approaching wedding. The daughters of Jerusalem are adorning the bride in her wedding apparel. As Solomon and his beloved gaze upon each other's beauty, the beloved finds herself lovesick and leans on the daughters of Jerusalem for strength. However, she is careful to ensure that this desire for Solomon does not lead her to improper sexual desire before she is married.

What does this text reveal about God's plan of salvation?

God created and instituted marriage in the Garden of Eden, uniting Adam and Eve as husband and wife into one flesh. Through His gift of marriage, God gives us a wonderful way to understand His love for us and the close relationship He wants to have with all His believers.

When we became estranged from Him by Adam and Eve's fall into sin, God promised to send His Son, and Jesus came on His mission to save us from our sin by paying the penalty by His death on the cross. Because He rose from the dead on the third day, He will return on the Last Day to raise the dead, to separate unbelievers from His Bride, the believers, and to bring us to live with Him in perfect bliss forever.

What does this text uncover about our identity and calling as God's people today?

God gifted humanity with sexuality, making a partner for Adam after declaring that it was not good for him to be alone. However, in Genesis and in the Ten Commandments, God clearly defines His plan for sexuality: that a man and woman should be bound together in the unity of marriage before they engage in sexual activity with each other. This text encourages us to flee from sexual temptation, not awakening our sexual desires until we are within the bounds of marriage.

As God's people, we are called to act differently and live to a higher standard than the people of this world. In a world of sexual freedom and promiscuity, our identity as God's people roots us in lives of sexual faithfulness and chastity.

SET THE SCENE

Betrothal and Marriage in the Bible

Traditional Israelite marriages were arranged by the fathers while the bride and groom were still children. When they reached the appropriate age, the two were betrothed. In this private ceremony, the man and woman exchanged vows and officially became husband and wife but did not live together or consummate their marriage (which explains why Joseph was prepared to divorce Mary when he found she was pregnant and knew he was not the father; see Matthew 1:18–21). The betrothal period usually lasted around a year as the husband prepared a home for his bride.

When the time for the wedding came, the bride and groom processed from the bride's house to the groom's house, where they consummated the marriage and a large banquet, lasting between one and two weeks, was hosted for guests.

This betrothal period in the marriage between Christ and His Bride, the church, fits our New Testament era very well. He is our husband and we are His Bride, but He has gone to prepare a place for us (see John 14:1–3). When the time is complete, Christ will return with His angels to take us to His home, the new heavens and the new earth, where we will live in glory and joy forever.

?

What comfort does understanding Jewish betrothal offer when we face persecution and suffering for the sake of Christ, our Groom, who rules at the Father's right side?

The Bride Adores Her Beloved (2:8–17)

The Song now cycles back in time to recall their courtship. The bride hears Solomon coming to court her and remind her that spring has come and the date for their wedding is drawing near. But Solomon and his beloved must first deal with the threats to their vineyard (v. 15) and to their marriage.

CLEAR THE CONFUSION

Why were Solomon and his beloved getting married again?

The Song of Solomon does not follow a linear progression through the traditional Israelite wedding process. If it did, it would begin with the courtship, followed by the wedding and finally the consummation. Instead, the Song begins at the end with the couple already married and having consummated their marriage. Now, in something like a flashback sequence, the Song presents the wedding process over and over in cycles as the poetry moves toward the reunion in the second half of the Song of Solomon.

The Bride's Dream (3:1–5)

Continuing in the courtship part of the cycle, the bride has a dream. It is unclear if the dream is verse 1 while verses 2–5 describe a subsequent midnight adventure or if the midnight search is part of the dream. In either case, the bride's desire for Solomon leads her to wander the city, searching desperately for him. When she finds him in verse 4, she intends to bring him into the house to consummate their marriage. But in verse 5, she interrupts herself, remembering she must resist the temptation to fulfill her sexual desire outside the bounds of marriage.

Solomon Arrives for the Wedding (3:6–11)

Now the cycle moves from courtship to wedding. With all the pomp and circumstance befitting a royal wedding, King Solomon and his beloved process in from the wilderness, surrounded by an entourage tasked with bearing and protecting the bride and groom. In verse 11, in the midst of this wedding, the daughters of Jerusalem are sent out to behold Solomon crowned in all his glory.

The language depicting columns of smoke coming up from the wilderness fits with the nation of Israel coming out from the wilderness to enter the Promised Land, led by the pillar of smoke and fire.

We might find Solomon's imagery difficult to understand because we don't live in the same culture. What phrases and images exist in our culture that would be difficult for someone in Solomon's culture to understand?

SET THE SCENE

Marriage and Matrimony in the Bible

In this wedding procession, the closest look at Solomon and his bride's wedding, we see many traditional Israelite wedding customs. First, the bride and groom were both perfumed with valuable fragrances. Next, the bride and the groom paraded through the city on elaborate litters and carriages. Solomon made the litter, a covered couch with elaborate curtains and carried on the shoulders of four men, for his beloved wife. He made his own carriage in a similar fashion to the temple, which he had built around the same time. Furthermore, the bride was accompanied by highly respected bodyguards, protecting the new queen of Israel. Finally, Solomon had been crowned for his wedding, a coronation that reaffirmed his authority.

LINK BETWEEN THE TESTAMENTS

The Wedding Procession of the King → Christ's Procession with His Bride (Song of Solomon 3:6–11 → Revelation 19:6–10)

The grand wedding of King Solomon points forward to the grand wedding between Jesus Christ and His Bride, the church, on the Last Day. Revelation 19:6–10 describes the marriage feast of Christ and the church. Just as a great multitude would have attended the royal wedding between King Solomon and his beloved, so the great multitude will attend the wedding of Christ the King. Christ presents His Bride, who is adorned in fine clothes just as Solomon's bride was adorned in expensive perfumes. This wedding serves as a recoronation for both Solomon and Christ, as all glory and honor is directed to Christ in His second coming. As the Bride of Christ, we eagerly await our awe-inspiring wedding, when we will be adorned in all splendor and be taken with Christ to the new creation.

VISUALIZE

Solomon's Wedding

Solomon Admires His Bride's Beauty (4:1–16a)

How is our love for family similar to our love for our spouse? How is it different?

Solomon proclaims the beauty of his beloved with vivid imagery, following the previous passage's description of the groom with a description of the bride in her adornment for the wedding. Solomon then invites his beloved to journey with him to Lebanon to live together there and consummate their marriage.

CLEAR THE CONFUSION

What do the images mean?

The metaphors and similes used to describe Solomon's bride, which conjure up confusing images rather than a beautiful bride, no longer make sense to modern audiences. With some explanation, modern audiences can understand the intentions of these unusual descriptions and develop a richer image of Solomon's beloved.

- "Your eyes are doves" (4:1). As the bride's face is veiled for the wedding, her eyelashes fluttering create the illusion of a dove's wings.
- "Your hair is like a flock of goats" (4:1). The imagery of jet-black goats streaming down a hillside is reminiscent of the bride's hair blowing in the wind.
- "Your teeth are like a flock of shorn ewes" (4:2). The dirty wool has been stripped off the sheep, leaving behind bright white lambs, paired ("twins") to emphasize the astounding symmetry of the bride's teeth.
- "Your lips are like a scarlet thread" (4:3). Bright red lips still serve as a sign of beauty in modern culture.
- "Your cheeks are like halves of a pomegranate" (4:3). Not only does a pomegranate have the redness of rosy cheeks, but pomegranates were also a symbol of fertility and righteousness in Israelite culture.
- "Your neck is like the tower of David, . . . on it hang a thousand shields" (4:4). The bride's straight and noble neck is adorned with necklaces, with bright, shining jewelry and ornamentation like newly polished shields. These necklaces were a key part of wedding regalia.
- "Your two breasts are like two fawns" (4:5). The softness of a fawn is present in Solomon's beloved.

LINK BETWEEN THE TESTAMENTS

A Locked Garden → The Garden with the River of Life (Song of Solomon 4:12 → Revelation 21)

While Solomon used the image of a locked garden to describe his bride's virginity in this passage, the Bible uses gardens to point us to creation and the new creation. The first humans, Adam and Eve, lived in the Garden of Eden in perfect union with God. When they sinned, the Garden of Eden became locked for all of humanity. In Revelation, God shows us the new creation, which will come on the Last Day. This new creation comes "prepared as a bride adorned for her husband" (Revelation 21:2), complete with a garden flowing with living water. While the Garden of Eden is locked to all humanity, the new garden will be opened to believers in the marriage feast between Christ and His Bride.

Together in the Garden of Love (4:16b–5:1)

WAYPOINT

What does this text show us?
The bride invites Solomon to unlock and enter the garden, previously established as a euphemism for the bride's virginity, thus consummating their marriage as bride and groom, who are intoxicated with holy sexual passion for each other.

The first half of the Song of Solomon takes us through cycles of poetry, drawing the reader through the courtship process and building to the wedding. At the center of the book, we see Solomon and his beloved's wedding, as the bride and the groom are described in all their splendor. The central event of the book occurs here, when Solomon and his bride consummate their marriage and begin new cycles exploring married love.

What does this text reveal about God's plan of salvation?
God's plan of salvation utilizes the beauty of sexual love and intimacy within marriage to help us understand God's desire to live in communion with all humans. Before Adam and Eve's fall into sin, God walked and talked intimately with them in the garden. He delighted in them, and they delighted in Him.

But when Adam and Eve sinned, they were driven out from God's presence and barred from Him. The only way to restore that intimate presence was for God to send His Son as the Groom, who went to search and find His lost Bride. Jesus took our guilt and sin upon Himself and paid the punishment for our sins when He died in our place on the cross. Risen in glory, now He prepares a place for us.

?

How does your understanding of God's gift of sex change when you recognize that God created sex for a husband and wife before sin entered the world?

?

Jesus describes eternity in the new heavens and the new earth as a wedding banquet. What impressions of our life in heaven does this imagery give to you? How do these increase your joyful anticipation of Christ's return?

When the Last Day comes, Jesus our Bridegroom will return to take His Bride—all believers—to live with Him once again in a new garden, the new heavens and the new earth. Then we will enjoy the consummation of our marriage to God forever and ever, exploring the wonders of our God and growing more and more delighted throughout all eternity.

How important is sex within a faithful Christian marriage?

What does this text uncover about our identity and calling as God's people today?
This text uncovers the proper role of sex within our lives as God's people, providing a positive example of God's wonderful gifts, which husbands and wives should aspire to. Our identity as Christians does not require sexual repression or celibacy, nor does it demonize proper sexual intimacy. Instead, we should develop the sexual dimension of our relationship with our spouse, rejoicing in the gifts God has given us and dutifully raising the children whom God chooses to give to us through this beautiful gift.

The Reunion in Married Love (5:2–8:14)

The final four chapters of the Song of Solomon explore the realities of married love as the bride and her beloved delight in each other, long for and search for each other, and reflect on the steadfastness of love.

The Bride Searches for Her Beloved (5:2–9)

In our human marriages, would this disinterest cause tension or conflict between a husband and wife? How is this tension or conflict normally resolved?

While Solomon's beloved is sleeping in her own chamber of the palace, Solomon comes to visit her. She initially is disinterested, focusing instead on her own comfort, but when her desire for him is aroused, she rushes to the door only to find that Solomon is gone. She searches the streets of the city for him but is beaten by the city watchmen and does not find her husband.

PICTURE OF THE SAVIOR

Spurning Our Bridegroom

These interactions between Solomon and his beloved point to our relationship with Christ as His beloved. We often find ourselves distracted or disinterested when Christ comes to us, just as Solomon's beloved did. Like her, we are focused on our own comfort and our own interests rather than listening to Christ's callings. We fail to follow Christ's commands to love our neighbors because we are comfortably lying on our proverbial beds, too tired to bother getting up. In the end, we spurn our Bridegroom, leaving Him to walk away dejected as Solomon did.

CLEAR THE CONFUSION

Why would the watchmen beat their king's beloved wife?

When the watchman encountered the bride on her earlier nightly search in the city (3:3–4), they helped her when she asked them in her search for Solomon. But this time they beat and bruised her, taking away her veil. Why?

Commentators have offered two basic answers. One is that the watchmen were evil; finding a helpless woman, they abused her physically if not sexually. But to keep the Eighth Commandment and explain everything in the kindest way, other commentators believe they mistook the king's bride for a prostitute or an adulteress who was prowling through the city streets at night, and they used force to keep her from committing a sin that would stir God's wrath against the holy city. Another explanation is that the watchmen recognized Solomon's bride and disciplined her for putting herself in harm's way because of her lovesick search for Solomon. This would parallel the anger of her brothers during her courtship when she neglected the family vineyard because she was distracted with love for Solomon (see 1:6).

The Bride Praises Her Beloved (5:10–6:1)

Having been questioned by the daughters of Jerusalem, Solomon's beloved recounts and describes his beauty, declaring his virtues and answering why he is better than any other groom. Notice that verses 10–11 give us a physical description of Solomon's appearance. His father, David, also had a ruddy or reddish complexion (1 Samuel 16:12).

?

If you are married, take a moment to consider the wonderful qualities of your spouse. If you are not married, think of someone special to you and do the same. Now think about Jesus' life, death, and resurrection. Take a moment to describe His wonderful qualities.

CLEAR THE CONFUSION

More images?

In a parallel to Solomon's previous praises, his beloved now praises him using similar metaphors, which may not make sense to modern audiences. With some explanation, modern audiences can understand the language and develop a richer image of Solomon.

- "My beloved is radiant and ruddy" (5:10). These words describe his overall appearance: Solomon has a red complexion, a color of life and vigor.
- "His head is the finest gold" (5:11). A golden tan still serves as a symbol of male beauty in modern culture.
- "His locks are wavy, black as a raven" (5:11). Raven is still a common descriptor of black hair with blue or green undertones.
- "His eyes are like doves . . . bathed in milk" (5:12). Similar to the bride's own eyes, the whites of Solomon's eyes are clear and bright, with a sparkle to them.
- "His cheeks are like beds of spices" (5:13). The raised garden beds reflect Solomon's high cheekbones, complete with the pleasing aroma of spices.
- "His lips are lilies, dripping liquid myrrh" (5:13). Solomon's lips are as delightful as lilies, and his breath is pleasant like the aroma of myrrh.
- "His arms are rods of gold, set with jewels" (5:14). Solomon's golden tan extends to his arms, with jewels inlaid in his bracelets.
- "His body is polished ivory, bedecked with sapphires" (5:14). This description refers to Solomon's plump belly, a cultural value in ancient Israel indicating that an individual was financially secure enough to obtain food and leisure. Solomon's torso is embellished with ivory and sapphires, highlighting his royal wealth.
- "His legs are alabaster columns" (5:15). This alludes to the two columns at the front of the temple, which Solomon built earlier in his reign. Solomon's legs are strong, yet beautiful, like the polished alabaster stone.
- "His appearance is like Lebanon" (5:15). Solomon's beloved adds a note of highly personal endearment, likening Solomon to Lebanon, the mountainous region near her hometown of Shunem.
- "His mouth is most sweet" (5:16). As Solomon's lips were praised earlier, the reference to Solomon's whole mouth draws attention to his impressive oratory skills.

Together in the Garden of Love (6:2–3)

WAYPOINT

What does this text show us?

After searching unsuccessfully for Solomon and recounting his beauty, his beloved realizes Solomon is returning to her garden, and there they reaffirm their devotion to each other.

Solomon's beloved struggles in their marriage, as she must reconcile her own self-centered desires with the duties she has to her groom. With the guidance of the daughters of Jerusalem, she rediscovers her love for Solomon and turns to the assurance of her marriage vows.

What does this text reveal about God's plan of salvation?

At times, we let earthly distractions and comforts drive our hearts and thoughts from our Lord and Savior. But Jesus steadfastly loves us and reaches out for us. He died for our sins and rose again to open the doors of eternal life in God's presence to all believers. Now He comes to us in Word and Sacraments to remind us of His love and to fill our hearts with yearning for His return.

What does this text uncover about our identity and calling as God's people today?

As God's people, we are called to let our lives shine as a light to the world so they might witness our conduct, listen to the Gospel, and be brought to faith (Matthew 5:16). This shapes our Christian identity as a living witness to the Gospel. In our marriages, we should also let our lives proclaim the steadfast promises of God: as God keeps all His promises to us, so we keep our marriage vows to our spouse.

?

With divorce being common in our society, how does the permanence in our wedding vows (for better or for worse, for richer or for poorer, in sickness and in health, until death parts us) change how we see marriage?

?

How does your faith toward Christ mirror the bride's wavering attitudes toward her groom? What has Christ provided to strengthen your bond to Him?

?

Does a broken promise make our future promises less trustworthy? Does a broken wedding vow?

PICTURE OF THE SAVIOR

I Am His and He Is Mine

In this brief passage, we witness the resolution of tension between Solomon and his beloved. When Solomon was spurned by his bride, he left and she could find him nowhere. She was distraught and enlisted the daughters of Jerusalem to aid in her search. The daughters of Jerusalem asked her leading questions so she would remember what made her groom so wonderful. This led the bride to renew her wedding commitment as she realized that Solomon would return. Solomon was hers, and he would remain steadfast to her no matter what.

The actions of Solomon point us forward to Jesus. We often spurn Him as we sin, refusing to open our hearts to Him. The actions of Solomon's beloved demonstrate the ideal response to such a situation: when we remember Jesus' love and mercy, we repent of our coldness and renew our faith, knowing that Christ has always remained steadfast to us.

Solomon and His Bride Delight in Each Other (6:4–7:10)

What about our sinful nature makes it important for husbands and wives to frequently show their devotion and love toward each other?

How is weekly worship a reminder of Christ's steadfast love as He comes again and again like a husband wooing his bride?

How does our restored relationship with Christ change the way we understand our faith?

What metaphors do poets use to describe their lovers today?

WAYPOINT

What does this text show us?

Reunited, Solomon delights in his bride, praising her as he did on their wedding day. Later, his beloved is swept away by Solomon's chariots, leading the daughters of Jerusalem to marvel and Solomon to praise her beauty once more.

As Solomon reconciles with his beloved, he rejoices in her presence and praises her beauty above all other women. After Solomon's beloved is swept away by the chariots of Solomon's entourage and the daughters of Jerusalem call to her, Solomon publicly declares her beauty and his desire for her.

What does this text reveal about God's plan of salvation?

Solomon and his beloved point forward to the relationship between Christ and His church. Although we spurn Christ, He seeks us out personally and restores our relationship with Him. He declares us to be righteous, giving us the righteousness He won on the cross.

What does this text uncover about our identity and calling as God's people today?

Because Christ's death on the cross atoned for our sins, He has restored our relationship with Him as His Bride. Our identity as the Bride of Christ calls us to love Him above all other things, proclaiming His deeds to the world as Solomon proclaimed his bride's beauty.

CLEAR THE CONFUSION

Even more images?

Once again, Solomon uses imagery to describe his beloved that no longer resonates with modern audiences. In fact, this passage contains two series of these metaphors. The first set of similes is an abridged version of Solomon's description of his bride in chapter 4 (for an explanation of these, see Clear the Confusion after 4:1–16a). The second set of imagery is explained below:

- "Beautiful as Tirzah . . . lovely as Jerusalem" (6:4). Tirzah was an important city in the northern part of Israel, where the Shulammite lived. After the kingdom of Israel was divided into two following Solomon's death, Tirzah served as the capital of the Northern Kingdom for over one hundred years before Ahab's father, Omri, made Samaria its capital (1 Kings 12–16). Of course, Jerusalem had the beautiful temple and Solomon's elegant palaces.

- "Your rounded thighs are like jewels" (7:1). The curvature of a woman's hips and thighs still serves as a beauty standard in modern culture. Solomon compares this beauty to the ornamentation with jewels a bride receives on her wedding day.
- "Your navel is a rounded bowl" (7:2). The navel, serving as an analog for her stomach, is plump just like Solomon's, meeting the Israelite beauty standard and demonstrating her security.
- "Your belly is a heap of wheat" (7:2). Solomon doubles down on this Israelite beauty standard, vividly demonstrating his beloved's abundance of provisions.
- "Your neck is like an ivory tower" (7:4). Solomon once again describes the strength and nobility of his bride's neck, using ivory as a comparison for her smooth complexion.
- "Your eyes are pools in Heshbon" (7:4). The sparkling, clear eyes of Solomon's beloved are reservoirs for tears and reminders of Israel's military victories in that city.
- "Your nose is like a tower of Lebanon" (7:4). The strong nose, in line with the beauty standards of ancient Israel, is reminiscent of Lebanon, the source of many choice materials for the temple and Solomon's palace.
- "Your head crowns you like Carmel" (7:5). The breathtaking beauty of her head reminds Solomon of the coastal views from Mount Carmel.
- "Your flowing locks are like purple" (7:5). The bride's hair is remarkable and precious, just like the rare purple tapestries and garments reserved for royalty.
- "Your stature is like a palm tree, and your breasts are like its clusters" (7:7). Throughout the Old Testament, palm trees represent life and salvation. The breasts, used for nursing infants, are the fruit by which she provides nourishment for her children.

Why is it important for husbands and wives to overlook each other's shortcomings? What will Christ do with our sinful shortcomings when He returns on the Last Day?

PICTURE OF THE SAVIOR

Jesus Dearly Loves His Bride

In Solomon's greatest love song, we see him imperfectly reflect the love of Christ for His Bride, the church. Chapters 6 and 7 recount how Solomon saw his new bride. He indulged in the most beautiful imagery and descriptive language when picturing her, clearly indicating his great love for her despite her low status as a Shulammite, working-class woman. Because of our sinful nature, we are a stained and broken people in the eyes of the Law. We deserve nothing but punishment. In His grace and mercy, however, Jesus saw past all our blemishes and died for us to clothe us anew in His righteousness—a finer garment than any lavish cloth described here. Solomon cherished his beloved above all else, taking great care to love her dearly as his wife and beloved. Jesus, having covered us in His righteousness, brings us into His heavenly kingdom by means of His Word and Sacraments, sustaining us in our eternal relationship with Him.

CLEAR THE CONFUSION

How do we know the Song of Solomon was written early in Solomon's reign?

In 6:8, we read that Solomon at this time had sixty queens and eighty concubines. Later in his reign, he had seven hundred wives and three hundred concubines, who turned his heart from God and undoubtedly from the Shulammite also.

The Bride Gives Her Love (7:11–13)

Looking for springtime signs of new life, Solomon's beloved invites him to the vineyards to share sexual intimacy as husband and wife. This is reminiscent of the Garden of Eden, where Adam and Eve lived as husband and wife, one flesh, and enjoyed intimate communion with God.

Our current culture encourages everyone to discover and express their own racial, sexual, and other identities. How is our baptismal identity similar to and different from other identities? How do we express this baptismal identity in our life?

Longing for Her Beloved (8:1–7)

Solomon's beloved expresses her desire for her husband, recalling the consummation of their marriage and reflecting on the strength and steadfastness of God's love and our love.

VISUALIZE

"Set me as a seal upon your heart." (Song of Solomon 8:6)

CLEAR THE CONFUSION

Why did the bride wish Solomon was like a brother?

In ancient Israel, it was not customary to express marital intimacy publicly (see Genesis 26:8, when Isaac and Rebekah share an intimate moment when they think they are unseen). But a sister could kiss her brother and no one would despise her. She wished to publicly show her love for her husband.

PICTURE OF THE SAVIOR

The Burning Passionate Flame

In an aside from the poetic narrative of the Song of Solomon, 8:6–7 presents a reflection on love itself. This passage shows us the steadfastness of love as it persists beyond death and withstands floods. It also shows the strength and passion of love, burning as bright as the flame of the Lord and driving men to sacrifice all the possessions they own.

The perfect love presented in this passage motivated Christ to die on the cross for His Bride, the church. In coming to earth, He offered all the wealth of His house and gave up His comfortable life in heaven, choosing to live an arduous life on earth as a human, where "He was despised and rejected by men" (Isaiah 53:3) and died for our sins. While human love is as strong as death, moving mankind to die for the people we love, Christ's divine love was stronger than death as He rose from the grave.

As the Bride of Christ, we also experience this love. In Baptism, the seal of the cross was placed upon our heads and our hearts. We were sealed as God's people, and God's name was placed upon our hearts. This is a love that will transcend death and the grave, as we will be gathered to Christ, our Bridegroom, when we die. The flame of the Lord appeared at Pentecost to mark the coming of the Holy Spirit, which is given to us personally through the waters of Holy Baptism. In response, we forsake the riches of this world as we "lay up for [ourselves] treasures in heaven" (Matthew 6:20).

Final Advice (8:8–14)

WAYPOINT

What does this text show us?

A group of brothers deliberate how they should protect their young sister's chastity, which prompts the bride to reflect on her own chastity. As Solomon and his bride manage their own vineyards, they share the profits in financial unity. Finally, the Song of Solomon closes with one last call of longing for each other.

Amid these numerous reflections in the Song of Solomon, we read about the importance of chastity, unity within marriage, and desire for one's spouse. In these reflections, we get a glimpse of God's plan for marriage and our relationship with Christ as His Bride.

?

In wedding vows, husband and wife promise to love each other "until death do us part." Compare this to God's love, which is stronger than death. What does this teach you about God's love?

What does this text reveal about God's plan of salvation?
God is passionate in His love for us. When we give our attention to other gods and withhold love and devotion from our God, He is filled with righteous jealousy and rage. God could have abandoned us and would have been in His proper rights to do so. But He so loved the world that He sent His only-begotten Son to die for us all. In Jesus, we are washed clean of our sin and made spotless and pure. When Christ returns, He will remove our sinful nature, and we will live in perfect love for God and for one another.

What does this text uncover about our identity and calling as God's people today?
God planned for marriage to be chaste, unifying, and a place for desire. God planned for sex to be a gift found solely within the bounds of marriage, between one man and one woman.

Likewise, God has planned for our worship to be located solely within the bounds of our relationship with Him, given to no other gods. God planned for husbands and wives to be unified in all aspects of their marriage, even financial aspects. As we grow in our relationship with God, we seek to become united with Him as we depend on Him for all things, including all our financial needs. Finally, God planned for the mutual desire between a husband and a wife to mirror His desire for us and the desire we should have for Him.

Our identity as God's people calls us to live unlike the rest of the world. We are called to live a chaste life and seek unity with our spouse in every aspect of our marriage. We must not be conformed to the ways of the world, but we must live out our identity as God's people so our lives can be a witness to all of the world.

In what ways do you have unity with your spouse? In what ways do you have unity with God?

How does our chastity serve as a witness that leads others to Christ?

SET THE SCENE

The Role of a Woman's Brothers in the Bible

In ancient Israel, a woman's brothers played a substantial role in her courtship and marriage process. Brothers were tasked with protecting their sister's virginity and were authorized to take vengeance on anyone who violated her. (Consider Jacob's sons, who avenged their sister Dinah's rape. At the same time, Jacob rebuked their excessive cruelty. See Genesis 34.) Brothers also actively participated in selecting their sister's husband, arranging her betrothal.

Why is protecting virginity important for an adolescent's mental and spiritual development?

CLEAR THE CONFUSION

Why were the brothers talking about walls and doors?

The brothers used walls and doors as metaphors for their sister's virginity. Because brothers were responsible for guarding their sister's virginity before marriage, these brothers deliberated how they should fulfill this obligation. The wall symbolized virginity, and if their sister was a virgin, the brothers would provide her with extra layers of protection that would also show her beauty. The door, being an entrance through a wall, symbolized promiscuity. If their sister had been promiscuous, the brothers planned to board up the door, preventing her from furthering her promiscuous lifestyle. After this deliberation from the brothers, Solomon's beloved remarked that she was a wall, meaning that she had remained a virgin until the consummation of her marriage with Solomon.

LINK BETWEEN THE TESTAMENTS

The Song's View of Marriage → The Christian Life Is Different (Song of Solomon 8:8–10 → Romans 12:1–2)

In Romans 12:1–2, Paul writes,

> I appeal to you therefore, brothers, by the mercies of God, to present your bodies as a living sacrifice, holy and acceptable to God, which is your spiritual worship. Do not be conformed to this world, but be transformed by the renewal of your mind, that by testing you may discern what is the will of God, what is good and acceptable and perfect.

Song of Solomon 8:8–10 presents a view of marriage that contradicts what the world tells us. We are told that virginity does not matter and that we should experiment with our sexuality to discover our sexual identity, and we are encouraged to have sex with others early in our lives so that we can be experienced enough to please our current sexual partner and our future spouse.

Paul warns us against following these ideals. While he is not primarily advocating for the importance of chastity in Romans 12, Paul teaches that the human body is holy to God and that we should support it with things that are good, acceptable, and perfect. Paul understands that this is at odds with the values of the world, so he encourages us not to follow the world's values but instead to follow God's values, including a sexually chaste life.